THE REGIMENT

Frontispiece – Trooper BSACP 1891

THE REGIMENT

A History and the Uniforms of the British South Africa Police

Richard Hamley

COVOS DAY

Published by Covos Day Books, 2000
Oak Tree House, Tamarisk Avenue,
P.O. Box 6996, Weltevredenpark 1715, South Africa

First published in 1971, by T.V. Bulpin and Books of Africa (Pty) Ltd as
The Regiment – The History and Uniform of the BSA Police
A Limited Edition of 350 copies, published in 1980, by Quest Publishing (Pvt) Ltd as
The Regiment

Cover design by JANT Design
Design and origination by JANT Design
+27 12 664-6340, email: j.design@mweb.co.za

Printed and bound by Creda Communications, Eliot Avenue, Epping II 7460

ISBN 0-620-25394-0

This book is dedicated to
the enduring memory
of the
British South Africa Police
and
all who wore its uniform
with pride

Pro Rege, Pro Lege, Pro Patria

Preface

While it may be a truism, it is nevertheless a fact that the history of the BSAP was that of Rhodesia itself—and the history of Rhodesia that of the British South Africa Police.

July 1966: – *'Sergeant Hamley, you will lecture recruits on the history of the Force.'*

Thus, in few words, was the Deputy Commandant of Tomlinson Depot*, the Training School for African Police, ultimately responsible for the production of this book.

At that time *"Your Force"* lectures to recruits were a new venture. Old hands in the BSAP were not formally taught the history of their Force. They began to assimilate it as they put their first foot within the confines of the Depot, ate their first meal in the Troops' Mess, or quaffed their first pint in the Regimental Institute. It is probably true to say that we learnt much more than we were taught in the Depot, and not only in matters pertaining to Force history: *'You're expected to be jacks of all trades, me lads,'* and, *'In the BSAP we turn our hands to anything.'* These were precepts imbued in us with our "Depot" haircuts—and on occasion we even did those ourselves!

With such precedent, and much like "Little Topsy", the lecture notes—and the aids used to stimulate interest on warm afternoons—have grown; have been re-drawn and drawn again, polished and re-fashioned until, finally, their author is satisfied that that which is presented is the best that an otherwise untutored policeman could produce.

The intention of *The Regiment*, in its various forms, has always been to encapsulate the proud history of the Corps in which the author had the honour to serve. And, at the same time, to provide an assemblage or more detailed history of the various uniforms of the Force—worn from its inception in 1890 to the stand-down in 1980—before all is lost to the mists of time and faulty recollection.

From the outset the methods used to compile this assemblage were those of an ordinary policeman conducting any inquiry or investigation. Doing this, in Rhodesia, one could rely on the whole-hearted support of public and officialdom alike.

In compiling the lecture notes, which formed the basis for the resulting manuscript, reference was made to the writings of Wilfred Bussey, the first editor of *The Outpost* (then entitled *The Police Review*); to Lieutenant-Colonel Colin Harding's *Frontier Patrols*, and to Colonel A.S. Hickman, MBE, Commissioner of Police from 1954 to 1955 and author of much Rhodesiana. Later polish was supplied by reference to the authoritative works of Peter Gibbs in *The First Line of Defence* and *The Right of the Line*.

---

* Chief Superintendent, later Assistant Commissioner, A.J. Sowter

The numerous illustrations in this book were drawn either from photographs of the period or from material found in the Rhodesian National Archives (later the National Archives of Zimbabwe), the Queen Victoria Museum, or from Police Sources such as the regimental magazine, *The Outpost*.

I was singularly fortunate in the help, advice and encouragement that I received from many sources. In particular I must renew my thanks to the late Mrs Ruth Whyte, the Curator and the Staff of what was then the Queen Victoria Museum; the Director and the Staff of the Rhodesian National Archives, and to my mentor the late Colonel A.S. Hickman. The late Captain "Teddy" Hughes Halls too was ever generous with his reminiscences of the early days of the Force—a dandy of his day, he served as the model for the trooper portrayed in Plate 12. Diana Mallet-Veale, an early Rhodesian water-colourist, provided the inspiration for Plate 19 and for the Auxiliary Policewoman in Plate 28. Chief Superintendent (Retd) A.C.N. [Steve] Stephens, unknowingly provided the model for the cover, and by the example of his own nautical research, encouraged me to write this book. Nicholas Gaskin taught a beginner how to paint and Paul Moorcraft struggled valiantly with my prose for the 1980 edition. To the latter—*"May* ***the Force*** *be with you"*.

My greatest indebtedness, of course, is to my wife Helen.

Richard Hamley
Willeton
Western Australia
March 2000

Foreword

It gives me great pleasure to write a foreword to Richard Hamley's book "The Regiment". During our years of war against terrorist incursions, I maintained close contact with our security forces, concious of the vital role which they were performing.

The BSAP enjoyed the reputation of being probably the finest police force in the world, going back to their formation in 1889. This great history obviously stimulated their performance, and this was never better demonstrated than the manner in which they responded to the demands made on them during our terrorist war. A large amount of our urban security responsibility was taken over by local civilians who were unavailable for active service. They were formed into Police Reserve units. This enabled BSAP members to take on military duties alongside army units. Police stations throughout the country became operation centres for all security forces. The BSAP continued their specialist duties in the fields of Intelligence, Special Branch, and Ground Coverage—this assumed even greater importance. A vital development was the formation of PATU – Police Anti-Terrorist Units. These multiracial units had a special facility for gaining the confidence of the local people, and thus their assistance in combating the evil of terrorism. I will not deal with the history of the BSAP, as this has been expertly covered by Richard Hamley.

It remains for me to congratulate him on his tremendous effort in recording for posterity this invaluable chapter of world history. Truely, a magnificent contribution.

The Honourable Mr. Ian Douglas Smith GCLM, ID
Harare
Zimbabwe
August 2000

List of Illustrations

Plates

Plate No	Title	Page

Sub-plates

The British South Africa Police

The territory at one time referred to geographically as *British South Africa*, was that area of land located between the Limpopo and Zambezi rivers, bounded in the east by the borders of Portuguese East Africa (Mozambique) and in the west by that of the Bechuanaland Protectorate (now Botswana), which was ceded to the British South Africa Company by Royal Charter in 1889. It should not be confused with that much larger country to the south of the Limpopo River, previously the Union and now the Republic of South Africa—which was never wholly *British* either in title or concept.

British South Africa was renamed *Rhodesia* in 1895. It became the Republic of Zimbabwe in August 1980.

It was the British South Africa Police—originally the British South Africa Company Police (BSACP)—that were responsible for bringing the rule of law to this portion of the dark continent.

The history of this distinguished paramilitary organization is in reality the history of five corps of police, each of which for a while having a separate existence under the banner of the British South Africa Company and then, in the fullness of time, amalgamating to become the national police service of Rhodesia.

It is a most unusual, if not a unique circumstance, for a police force to be established before the country—that it is to watch and have ward over—formally came into existence. Nevertheless, this is what happened, in the context of that which was to be known as *the scramble for Africa*.

The complexities of local and international politics, commercial intrigue and the inevitable machinations of expansionism which surround this issue, are such as to have filled many a historical treatise and thus require far greater attention than is possible within the confines of this work. It is, however, necessary to make passing reference to the acquisition of the Bechuanaland territories, and to the establishment of the Bechuanaland Protectorate itself, in order to bring matters into perspective and to provide a starting point for the narrative that follows.

THE BECHUANALAND TERRITORIES were declared a British Protectorate on May 21st 1884. Six weeks later, on July 1st, a force of 100 men, predominantly of British origin, was assembled and organized to police the new territory. Their jurisdiction, however, was limited to that area lying to the north of Griqualand West and south and east of the Mtopo River, later to be the Colony of British Bechuanaland and later still to become part of the Republic of South Africa.

The so-named *Bechuanaland Mounted Police* lacked strength on the ground properly to control the incursions of the numerous adventurers operating out of the neighbouring Boer Republics, who were becoming not only a cause for local concern but also a threat to British authority in Southern Africa generally. The Imperial Government, considerably alarmed by the recent German annexation of South West Africa and constantly prompted by the indefatigable Cecil Rhodes, sent a military expedition under Sir Charles Warren to restore order in the region.

At the conclusion of this none-too-exacting campaign, Lieutenant-Colonel Sir Frederick Carrington, late 24th Regiment, South Wales Borderers, was charged with raising a new force of police to defend the territory. On 4th August 1885, the *Bechuanaland Border Police* (BBP) was established with recruits to be drawn, in the main, from men who had served in Warren's Field Force (including time-expired personnel from the Cape Mounted Rifles) and the Bechuanaland Mounted Police.

Enrolment for the Bechuanaland Border Police commenced at Barkly West, near Kimberley, on 15th August 1885. By 28th August, Carrington had at his disposal a select corps comprising 477 non-commissioned officers and men, well mounted and well armed and soon to become disciplined into a force that was to combine the duties of police, mounted infantry, light cavalry and, on occasion, light artillery.

Garrisons were established at Taungs, Vryburg and Mafeking and a number of other points along a 400-mile frontier from whence the corps issued to provide protection to the territory's inhabitants, maintain communications, function as veterinarians and act as diplomats and arbitrators in tribal matters and disputes over water rights to the remote wells and water holes scattered over the arid Kalahari.

The Bechuanaland Border Police were instrumental not only in safeguarding the Bechuanaland Protectorate against Freebooters and incursions by the Boers, but for paving the way for the 1890 Pioneer Column's expedition to Mashonaland. In providing a significant portion of the escort that was to accompany the Column, the BBP have to be considered as the principal progenitor of the British South Africa Police.

Plate 1. The Bechuanaland Border Police: Trooper 1889

The genesis of the British South Africa Police can be dated back to 15th August 1885, when enrolment commenced at Barkly West (near Kimberley) for the Corps that was to be identified as The Bechuanaland Border Police. The Warren Expedition had recently completed its task of pacifying the no man's land located in the region where the frontiers of the Cape Colony, the Transvaal (South African Republic) and the Bechuanaland Territory converged.

Colonel Frederick Carrington commanded the new force. Its members, for the most part rugged individualists, attracted to the prospect of an adventurous, action-packed life in the open air. Many had been in the bush for years and knew the ways of the veldt, both as hunters and prospectors. Some were men of good family, well educated and cultured. Only the best were selected for a Corps which was to gain a solid reputation for its high standard of discipline and personal behaviour.

The Trooper illustrated is shown wearing uniform and equipment common to the Corps at the time of its first association with the British South Africa Company.

A number of sources have it that the brown slouch hat was worn turned up on the right side. Photographic evidence, however, is inconclusive. Certainly there are grounds to believe that, apart from the matter of the puggaree, the headgear of the Bechuanaland Border Police conformed to that worn by the British South Africa Company Police when they served together as part of the Company's forces.

As was the case later with the BSACP, ordnance was drawn from stores in Kimberley and apparently there was some variation in the style of uniforms supplied. The tunic, generally, was of dark brown corduroy with either twisted black shoulder cords or plain straps of self-material. The frock had pouch breast and skirt pockets, sometimes covered by flaps. Brass "Imperial" buttons were often (but not always) worn on tunic fronts. Differing styles of tunic, in the same material, were fastened with hooks and eyes. A brown leather bandolier, black leather (snake-fastening) belt, long blue puttees and black ankle boots completed the ensemble. A second uniform of khaki twill was issued, as were cavalry cloaks.

From an examination of early photographs it would appear that officers wore a similar brown cord tunic with lighter brown cord or doeskin breeches; a black leather Sam Browne; knee boots and hunting spurs. As an alternative to the slouch hat, a dark brown forage cap, without buttons at the front, was worn.

The Bechuanaland Border Police were finally absorbed into the British South Africa Company forces toward the end of the year 1896 becoming No. 1 Bechuanaland Protectorate Division of the British South Africa Police.

No. 1 Division of the British South Africa Police was disbanded with the reorganization of the Company's police forces in 1903.

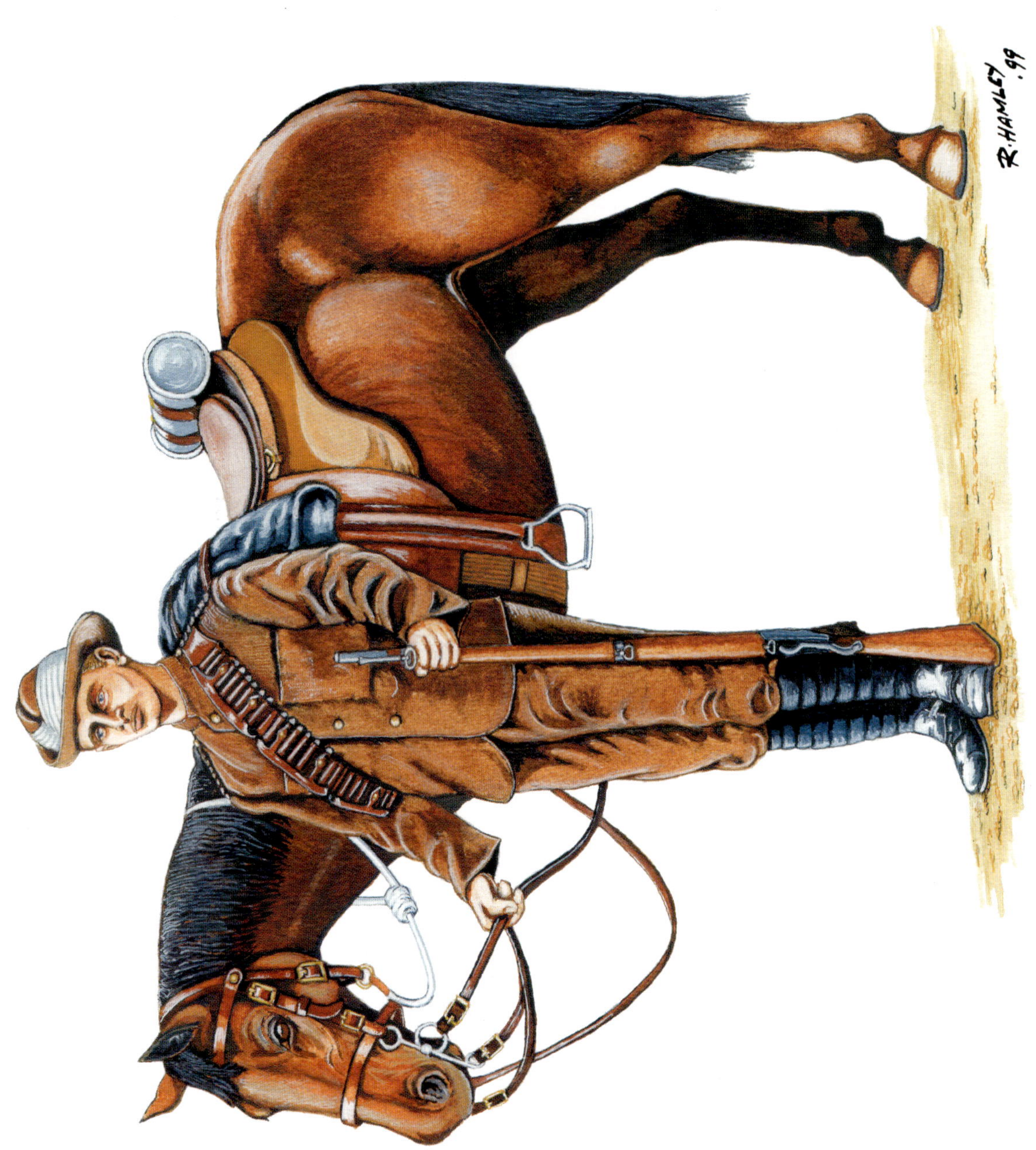

Plate 1

Plate 2. The Pioneer Corps: Officer 1890

The story of the 1890 Pioneers and the Pioneer Column is too well documented elsewhere to warrant repetition in this work. It is enough to record that some 180 very carefully selected men were recruited by Major Frank Johnson[1] at Kimberley, on behalf of the British South Africa Company, to form a semi-military Corps of Pioneers to go to Mashonaland where, upon disbandment, they would colonize the territory.

Johnson was contracted by the British South Africa company to recruit, provision and equip a body of men to make a good wagon road from Palapye in Bechuanaland to Mount Hampden in Mashonaland, the intended destination of the expedition. His force, assisting the Police, was to occupy and hold the new territory until they were relieved of this responsibility on 30th September 1890. Thereafter, upon relinquishing their military role, the Pioneers became the country's first white settlers.

Frank Johnson chose his men mainly from among the miners of the Transvaal: tough, hard-working individuals who could wield both gun and pick with equal aplomb and live as roughly as the occasion demanded. As was their leader, the recruits were given temporary military rank and status. They were divided into three troops: two of mounted infantry and the third, an artillery troop, which was equipped with 7-pound cannon and quick-firing Maxims. The Corps went into training alongside the British South Africa Company Police at MacLoutsie.

On 13th June 1890, both Pioneers and Police were inspected by Major General Lord Methuen, the Adjutant general of British Forces in South Africa, and declared *ready in all respects* for the task ahead. They commenced the great trek northwards, entering what was to become Rhodesia on 6th July 1890. Fort Salisbury was reached on 12th September 1890. The following day the British flag was hoisted and possession taken of the territory in the name of Queen Victoria.

The Pioneer Column remained as one force until 1st October 1890, when the Pioneers, having fulfilled their contract by constructing a fort, disbanded to seek their fortunes elsewhere.

The Pioneers did not turn up the sides of their slouch hats as did contemporary units, and their puggarees appear to have been many and varied, often of guinea-fowl pattern, but most commonly of white material. The tunic of an officer was dark brown cord with black facing braid. His shoulder cords, solid silhouette "Austrian knots" and rank badges were similarly blue/black. Riding breeches have been described as either grey or yellow (brown) cord. Leggings, ankle boots with hunting spurs and a Sam Browne, complete with holster and ammunition pouch, constituted the leatherwork worn by officers. Not surprisingly, the leather did not display a high degree of *spit and polish*. Other ranks of the Pioneer Corps were similarly attired, but wore a brown leather

---

1 Former BBP Quartermaster Sergeant, adventurer, prospector and friend of Rhodes.

Plate 2

bandolier instead of a belt. NCO rank badges appear to have been off-white tape upon a black or dark blue background.

The Maxims of C troop, the artillery of the Pioneers, were handled by a detail of naval blue-jackets; which would seem to account for the appearance in many old photographs of the Royal Navy's striped jersey of that period.

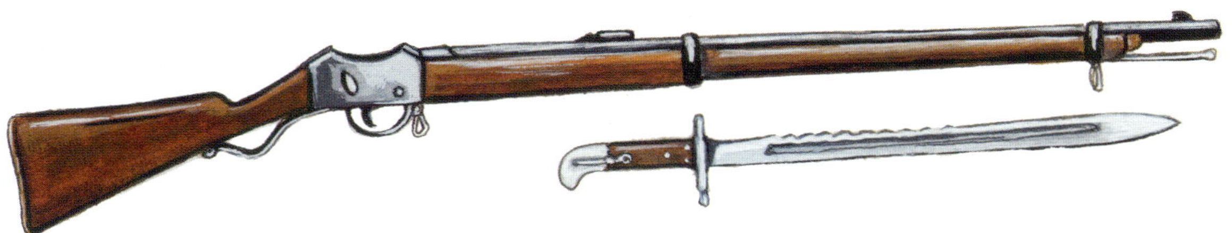

Martini-Henry Rifle and Bayonet

ON THE STRENGTH of a concession to *win and procure metals* obtained by the adventurer, Charles Rudd, from Lobengula, Paramount Chief of the Ndebele nation, Rhodes's newly formed British South Africa Company successfully petitioned Queen Victoria to grant a Royal Charter empowering it to occupy and to exploit the territory lying to the north of Bechuanaland and to the west of Portuguese East Africa. The granting of this Charter on 15th October 1889 and the subsequent organizing of a Pioneer Corps by Frank Johnson also saw the birth of the British South Africa Company's Police. For along with the commercial undertakings, sanctioned by the Charter, the Company was at the same time and to the best of its ability, to *preserve peace and order*. For this purpose it was authorized to establish and maintain a police force.

The British Government was adamant that any column of so-called pioneers or first settlers had to be provided with an adequate military escort. They were equally adamant that such escort should not, either in fact or by any fiction, be seen as, or be interpreted as being, an *Imperial* military force. So it was that the *British South Africa Company Police* came into existence with the configuration of a small regiment of cavalry.

The majority of the force raised to provide this military escort was drawn from personnel retrenched by the BBP, which was reduced in strength for this purpose. The Company's Police were encamped near the BBP Camp at MacLoutsie where, under the command of Lieutenant-Colonel S. G. Pennefather, formerly 6th Inniskilling Dragoons, it rapidly grew in strength to five troops. By the middle of June 1890, the Police and Pioneers were considered ready to undertake the task ahead of them. Major-General Methuen, the Adjutant General of British forces in South Africa, inspected them, watching a sham fight between the Company's Police and the BBP and the formation at speed of a defensive wagon laager. He was pleased to pass them as *ready in all respects for duty*.

On 6th July the combined force crossed the Shashi River to set out for their final destination—the yet to be located, Fort Salisbury. Notwithstanding the show of military force, but faced with the prospect of becoming embroiled with a warrior nation, the Company took the marginally softer option of heading north-eastward to the country of the *Vashona*.

As the column progressed, troops of police were left en route to establish and garrison forts and to maintain the lines of communication. Of the five troops of Police, one was left at Macloutsie, another took over garrison duty at Fort Tuli, while the other three escorted the Pioneers on the long ride that was to end with the establishment of Fort Salisbury.

At Fort Salisbury, on 13th September 1890, in the place that was to become the city centrepiece of Cecil Square, the Union Jack was raised and in the name of Queen Victoria, formal possession was taken of the territory.

Plate 3. The British South Africa Company Police: Trooper 1890

The granting of the Charter to Rhodes's British South Africa Company and the forming of the Pioneer Corps by Frank Johnson, also brought about the creation of the British South Africa Company's Police. More rugged individualists volunteered for this force and to their ranks also were transferred about half the strength of the Bechuanaland Border Police. From the beginning, therefore, the British South Africa Company Police inherited both the experience and equipment of the older force that was its progenitor.

As Wilfred Bussey, the editor of *The Police Review*[2], said in his history of the BSAP: *...the British South Africa Company's Police were assimilated to the Bechuanaland Border Police from the start...* Thus many items of uniform became common to both in the years that followed, and this is borne out by photographic record. Photographs also confirm that the standard dress of the British South Africa Company Police was the same as that pictured in reproduction of the Diana Mallet Veale[3] watercolour that appeared in the *Jubilee* issue of *The Outpost* in 1940:

> Bechuanaland Border Police pattern brown slouch hat, with green puggaree, fastened on the left side with the Police badge. This badge, which was very rough and ready in design, was of cloth and portrayed a lion bearing a tusk over the word "Police" and encircled by the Company's title, machine sewn in red upon a dark blue background. The tunic, of light brown corduroy, had brass "Company" buttons, pouch pockets at the breast, flap pockets on the frock, and yellow and red twisted shoulder cords. Breeches were of the same material as the tunic. A brown leather bandolier, S belt and knee boots completed this hardwearing and practical uniform.

Like his contemporary in the Bechuanaland Border Police, the Company's Trooper was armed with a Martini-Henry rifle, a weapon commonly used by both British and colonial forces. A single-loading breechloader of .45 calibre, its action was a falling breechblock activated by a lever on the underside. Sighted to 1,450 yards, the rifle fired a solid lead bullet. While it was a reasonably effective weapon of its era, it suffered principally from the fault of bad extraction. The sword bayonet used with the Martini-Henry was some 18 inches long. It was suspended from the *S* belt by a frog of ordinary infantry pattern but two inches longer in the strap in order that the bayonet might hand more easily when a man was mounted.

---

2 The forerunner of *The Outpost* – the Regimental Magazine of the British South Africa Police.

3 Early Rhodesian water-colourist and wife of Trooper Mallet Veale (BSACP).

Plate 3

THE PIONEER COLUMN and its Police escort remained together until 1st October 1890 when the Pioneers, having fulfilled their contract by the building of Fort Salisbury, disbanded to seek their fortunes elsewhere in the country. A town began to grow up around the police camp and the BSACP extended their operations to provide protection for the farmers and miners who spread out from this base. During the last few months of 1891, however, the Company came to the conclusion that it was uneconomic to maintain a large standing body of police. In January 1892, it retrenched the greater portion of the force, reorganizing the remaining 150 men into troops of the *Mashonaland Mounted Police*. It was intended that any *military* duties that might thereafter be occasioned should be undertaken by the so-designated *Mashonaland Horse*, a unit of volunteers raised with the help of the Company to protect the district against marauding Ndebele.

Men stood down from the BSACP were understandably angry, suggesting that members of the Mashonaland Horse had been duped into performing without recompense, duties that they previously had been paid to do. Certainly it seemed that the Company wished to have the best of both worlds, for although the Mashonaland Mounted Police were deemed a *civil* force, it was organized on the basis of a cavalry regiment that could be rapidly expanded should the need arise.

And such need did indeed arise when Lobengula, no longer able to restrain his impis from indulging in their former habit of raiding the Shona tribes, allowed a large army to cross the border into Mashonaland in July 1893—an event that led directly to the Company's invasion and annexation of Matabeleland.

Hat Badge – British South Africa Company Police

Plate 4. The Mashonaland Mounted Police: 1892 – 1896

In January 1892, the British South Africa Company disbanded the majority of its Police. The remainder (the number of 150 is mentioned in Harding's *Frontier Patrols*) were re-organized as a civil force: the Mashonaland Mounted Police. The military duties of the old Company's Police were to be undertaken, where necessary, by the Mashonaland Horse, a unit of volunteers raised with the aid of the Company to protect the territory against marauding Ndebele. Men retrenched from the Company's Police were understandably angry. They considered that the Mashonaland Horse had been duped and were performing, for nothing, duties that the old police had been paid to do.

It appeared that the British South Africa Company really did intend to have the best of both worlds, for although the Mashonaland Mounted Police were termed a "civil" force, it was organized on the basis of a small cavalry regiment, an organizational unit that could be rapidly expanded should the need arise. Such need did arise when Lobengula, unable to restrain his impis any longer from raiding the Shona tribes, allowed a large army to cross the border in July 1893. This foray led in turn to the invasion of Matableleland.

The uniform of the Mashonaland Mounted Police (MMP) inherited a great deal from a much older regiment—the Cape Mounted Rifles (formerly the Frontier Armed and Mounted Police of the Cape Colony). The tunic (and in the case of other ranks, their breeches) was of very dark grey, almost black, pepper and salt, bedford cord. Officers' breeches were of light tan or grey cord. Whilst it is apparent that a light grey felt hat, turned up at the left side and fastened with the MMP badge, was worn on occasions by officers, reference to photographic records shows that the use of the field service cap was more common.

The MMP badge was in white metal and of a neat rather classical design. It was worn without backing material. It would also seem to have been worn more by officers than by other ranks, probably owing to cost or lack of availability.

Field boots with straight hunting spurs and for officers, gauntlets, sword scabbard and their Sam Browne, were of black leather. A small ammunition pouch attached to the brace of the Sam Browne was a common feature.

Cap Badge – Mashonaland Mounted Police

Plate 4

THE DIVISIONS WHICH had arisen as a result of the raising of the first of Rhodesia's many volunteer units, the Mashonaland Horse, were soon swept aside in what was to be called the first Matabele War. Following a confrontation with a marauding impi near Fort Victoria, it was clear to the settlers that the time had come to teach the Ndebele a sharp lesson. Volunteers rallied to the Company flag to be formed into military units for an invasion of Matabeleland.

While the Company's police provided the nucleus of the forces to enter Matabeleland and the Bechunaland Border Police assisted as well, it was volunteer units or *Burgher* forces that made up the bulk of the invasion force. Four columns, each of 250 men supported by Maxims, were assembled; two from Mashonaland: the Salisbury Horse and the Victoria Rangers—and from the south: Commandant Raaf and his Rangers, the BBP and 1,800 mounted Bechuanas under their King—*Khama*.

Both sides fought with considerable courage and ferocity in an arduous campaign that lasted from October to December 1893. It was during this struggle that one of the most glorious episodes in early Rhodesian history took place, when Major Allan Wilson and 34 men of the Victoria Rangers met their end in a valiant last-stand near the Shangani River.

Nevertheless, before the end of the year the Ndebele were, to all intents and purposes, broken. Their King Lobengula had fled and died in the northern wilderness. Matabeleland was incorporated into a colony, first known as Southern Zambesia—shortly afterward Southern Rhodesia—and the settler town (later the city) of Bulawayo was established upon the site of Lobengula's kraal.

With the end of the War and the apparent subjugation of the Matabele, the Volunteer Units were disbanded, many of their number taking up grants of land in the conquered territory. A new regular force of police was formed, in association with its counterpart in Mashonaland, as a division of the Company's Police to be known as the *Matabeleland Mounted Police*. Its duties also were primarily military and intended to protect the settlers from the stray bands of hostile Ndebele that still lurked in areas around the Matopos, and the Shangani.

In the meantime *Town Police*—the *Mashonaland Constabulary* and the *Matabeleland Constabulary*—were formed in 1892 and 1893 respectively, the majority of recruits having been found within the ranks of Britain's Metropolitan Police and the Royal Ulster Constabulary. The two Constabularies remained in being, but separately administered, until amalgamated as the *Southern Rhodesia Constabulary* in 1903.

Plate 5. The Mashonaland Constabulary: 1892 – 1903

As in the case of the Mashonaland Mounted Police, there is a dearth of information regarding Rhodesia's first force of Town Police. An estimated date of its formation is early in 1892, about the same time that the Mashonaland Mounted Police was established. Otherwise known as the Municipal Police, the Mashonaland Constabulary could be described as Rhodesia's first truly civilian police force. Though the small mounted section which patrolled the outer fringes of the Municipal area was armed with .45 calibre revolvers, their colleagues covered the townships on foot and by bicycle, equipped only with a torch, handcuffs and a baton for self-protection. Its membership drawn principally from the police forces of the United Kingdom, this minuscule force remained in being until it was amalgamated with the Matabeleland Constabulary to form the Southern Rhodesia Constabulary in 1903.

The illustration portrays a sergeant major of the Town Police during the period 1890 to 1900:

> Blue tunic, probably serge, braided across the chest in a lighter blue; with blue facings on the collar and skirt; solid silhouette *Austrian Knots* on sleeves, the whole fastened with hooks. Blue trousers had turn-ups. The blue Austrian cap gave way to the most unglamorous peaked cap about the turn of the century. A chinstrap resting upon the cap badge appears to have been an affectation peculiar to Senior NCOs. Chevron lace would seem to have been gold upon dark blue or on occasions gold upon a deep red backing. All leatherwork was black.

A constable of Town Police wore the same uniform as the NCO but with no braiding across the chest and without a badge on the Austrian cap.

Mounted Section NCOs also wore the dark blue braided tunic with Austrian knots upon the sleeve, but differed from the Foot Branch in wearing a dark blue forage cap with two-button front, drab bedford cord breeches and dark blue puttees. The uniform of a constable in the Mounted Section was the same as that of the NCO but it had no braiding on the tunic.

> Police General Order No. 544 dated 28th May 1900 states:
>
> *The Commandant-General has approved of the uniform hereunder laid down for the officers of the Mashonaland Constabulary:*
>
> ***Full Dress:***
>
> *Dark blue patrol jacket, cavalry pattern, standing collar, braided according to rank. Dark blue serge overalls braided with two-inch black oak-leaf braid. Half-Wellington boots, box spurs and brown dog skin gloves—OR WHEN MOUNTED—khaki Bedford cord pantaloons (no braid), black butcher boots, steel spurs (hunting pattern) with chains.*

Undress:

Dark blue serge frock, four outside flap pockets, standing collar. Overalls, same as in full dress, pantaloons, boots and spurs same as full dress...

The Order goes on to state: ... *Officers visiting out-stations may wear khaki serge.* It describes the buttons of the undress uniform as: *bronzed and stamped with the Rhodesia Coat of Arms*; the shoulder belt as: ... *patent leather with silver-plated whistle and socket*; the pouch as: ... *patent leather bearing silver monogram*. The helmet is described as: *White doeskin helmet, cavalry pattern, white puggaree, black chinstrap, no spike and no badges*.

Brass Badge or Escutcheon – Mashonaland Constabulary

Plate 5

Plate 6. The Volunteers : 1893

Rhodesia's first volunteer unit was the Mashonaland Horse, whose formation in 1892 had been the cause of so much dissatisfaction among men disbanded from the British South Africa Company's Police. The first Matabele War, however, which erupted as a result of the butchering of Shona tribes-people in the *Victorian Massacre* and the subsequent confrontation with the Fort Victoria Police (in what became known as *the Lendy Affair*) swept aside such concerns.

It was soon a consensus that the time had come to teach the Ndebele a sharp lesson. Volunteers rallied to the call to arms and were formed into military units for the invasion of the Matabele kingdom.

The Matablele War involved just about every able-bodied white man in the country. While it was the Company's police providing the nucleus of the forces that were to enter Matabeleland and the Bechunaland Border Police assisted as well, it was the volunteer units or *Burgher* forces that made up the bulk of the invasion force.

Four columns, each of 250 men supported by Maxims, were assembled; two from Mashonaland: the Salisbury Horse and the Victoria Rangers; and from the south: the Afrikaner Commandant Raaf and his Rangers, the Bechuanaland Border Police and 1,800 mounted Bechuanas under their King—*Khama*. With such array of strength and sophisticated weaponry, a brief campaign was over by the end of November 1893.

Following what was perceived as a successful outcome, the Volunteer Regiments were disbanded on 23rd December 1893.

As volunteers were hurriedly called up, the uniforms adopted were many and varied with men wearing, in the main, what was left to them of the old Company's Police and Pioneer uniforms. The Volunteer Trooper depicted is shown as wearing a brown felt hat with a blue polka dot or guinea fowl pattern puggaree. His *grey-back* shirt and brown cord pantaloons, together with a tunic of the same material were probably drawn from Company stocks. A bandolier, *S* belt and field boots were all items of common issue. Although doubtless used earlier, it is at this period that a form of haversack for small kit and extra ammunition is noticeable in photographs.

Bandolier and Water Bottle (circa 1890)

Plate 6

Plate 7. The Matabeleland Mounted Police: 1893 – 1896

By the end of November 1893, the Matabele War was over. Matabeleland had been taken over by the British South Africa Company. Lobengula's principal kraal had been levelled and was being replanned as a European township. The Ndebele had been defeated but were still full of fight. Lobengula himself, fleeing northward in a bullock cart, died and was buried by his faithful indunas in a cave on a lonely hillside. In close pursuit, Allan Wilson and the 33 men of his patrol had been ambushed and died in what was to be immortalized as—*the last stand on the Shangani*. While this was going on, prospectors and the land-hungry spread out through the newly acquired territory in search of workable mines, farms and otherwise exploitable land.

To maintain law and order, a new regular force of police was formed. In association with the old Mashonaland Mounted Police and as part of the BSA Company's Police, it was to be known as the Matabeleland Mounted Police. Collectively the two forces were known as the MMP.

It was the young men of the Matabeleland Mounted Police who provided the greater number of the troops involved in the ill-fated Jameson Raid.

The uniform of the Matabeleland Mounted Police was of the same dark blue-black bedford cord as the Mashonaland Mounted Police. Early photographs indicate that drab cord breeches were also worn together with black knee boots or dark puttees as the occasion demanded. On the raid to Krugersdorp, the Matabeleland Mounted Police wore a grey felt hat pinned up at the left side and ornamented with the regimental badge. Their more usual headgear, however, was the field service cap. This cap was of dark blue cloth with a scarlet insert in the dented crown. Piping around the crown and flaps was of the same bright red colour. It seems that other ranks of the Matabeleland Mounted police were not in the habit of wearing their regimental cap badge—again, perhaps, because of a paucity of supply—but when they did do so it was with a backing of red cloth. Brass "Company" buttons were worn by both wings of the Mounted Police and an inverted white chevron worn on the left arm just below the elbow denoted a man who had re-engaged after two years' service.

The Mashonaland and Matabeleland Mounted Police were amalgamated as the Rhodesia Mounted Police on 1st October 1896.

Cap Badge – Matabeleland Mounted Police

Plate 7

FOR A SPACE of almost two years following the conclusion of the Matabele War, peace reigned throughout the territories administered by the British South Africa Company. In this period little of any note happened to Rhodesia's Police until the misadventure of the Jameson Raid.

Leander Starr Jameson, former medico, amateur soldier and principal co-founder of the BSA Company had, with some vicissitude, become even more prominent in the Company hierarchy, eventually holding the titles of Administrator of Mashonaland and Matabeleland as well as that of Resident Commissioner of Southern Bechuanaland.

Upon the cession of *British Bechuanaland* to the Cape Colony, Rhodes had persuaded the Imperial Government to cede a strip of land within the Bechuanaland Protectorate and running along the border with the Transvaal, to the British South Africa Company, ostensibly to provide for the construction of a railway line to the Cape. This was to be the starting point for the great adventure.

The period immediately before the raid was marked by considerable unrest in the gold mines around Johannesburg. Tales of flagrant injustice and oppression by the Boers (many of which were greatly exaggerated) reached Jameson from Britishers in the Transvaal. Their appeal for help, supported by promises of assistance, was enough to galvanize the energetic doctor—an ardent supporter of Rhodes's Cape-to-Cairo policy—into action. Accordingly, on 29th December 1895, from camps at Pitsani and Mafeking, he led a force of 511 men of the Mashonaland and Matabeleland Mounted Police, their ranks swelled by men disbanded from the Bechuanaland Border Police (including two troops still officially BBP), over the Border and into the Transvaal. They made a forced march of some 300 miles to Krugersdorp just outside Johannesburg. At nearby Doornkop, however, they were surrounded by a superior force of some 4,000 Boers who were supported by artillery. The help promised by the *Uitlanders*[1] failing to materialize, the Rhodesian forces were ultimately overwhelmed and taken prisoner.

The Jameson Raid was rightly termed a fiasco. A fiasco that led not only to the Ndebele and Shona rebellions but, indirectly, to the Boer War. However, that was the responsibility of the leaders and instigators of this incursion. Nothing can detract from the extraordinary courage and endurance shown by the troops involved, many of whom were little more than boys with no prior military experience.

Perusal of Regimental Orders shows that orders for both the Mashonaland and the Matabeleland Mounted Police ceased on 31st October 1896 and that both regiments had amalgamated as the *Rhodesia Mounted Police* with effect from 1st October that year.

---

1 Literally—*foreigners*

Plate 8. The Matabeleland Constabulary: Inspector 1895

This, the second of Rhodesia's entirely civilian police forces, was formed at the end of the Matabele War when Lobengula's kingdom was incorporated into British South Africa Company territory. Another *Municipal Police*, its organization was patterned upon that of the Mashonaland Constabulary and its duties, similarly, were those that concerned the policing of townships.

As is the case with the Mashonaland Constabulary, early records provide little information about the ten-year life span of this small unit. There is, however, little doubt that in terms of pure police-work the constabularies exhibited far more professionalism than did their colleagues of the BSAP. The latter were more inclined to view their role as that of mounted infantry or light cavalry and the mundane tasks of a constable were something of an anathema. A great deal of the constabularies' expertise had been derived from members' previous service with London's Metropolitan Police or the Royal Irish Constabulary. It was probably that same professionalism that led to a seeming unpopularity; for if nothing else, the early Rhodesian was noted for his rumbustious behaviour and like most colonials, hated to be socially constrained.

Some members of the BSAP, however, were products of British public schools. This might explain a somewhat snobbish attitude toward the Town Police. Nevertheless, the two constabularies must have done a very good job notwithstanding their social origins, for when in the late 1890s the BSAP were actively engaged in military duties elsewhere, peace and good order reigned at home.

From within the ranks of the Constabularies came such specialized units as the Criminal Investigation Department (CID), Traffic Police and incipient Dog Sections.

The officer illustrated is shown as wearing a dark blue cloth patrol jacket with five rows of fall mohair braid at the chest and olivets at the points. The jacket had a military collar with tracing braid, mohair braid at edges and back, plain sleeves with tubular braid mohair and Austrian-knots with bullet eye loops and tracing braid on the back. Chief Inspectors wore the same uniform distinguished by appropriate rank badges. A Sub-Inspector's jacket, however, had Austrian knots without bullet eye loops or tracing braid. Overalls were of the same blue cloth as the tunic and worn with oak-leaf braid on the side seams. The cavalry pattern helmet was of white doeskin with white metal spike and chain and white puggaree. Black half-wellington boots had block fronts and sprung sides and were worn with either swan-neck or straight hunting spurs. The cross belt was of black enamelled leather and carried a white-metal pouch at the rear and a white metal whistle fitted into an ornamental socket attached by a chain to a lion's head plug at the front. Gloves were either of white doeskin or tanned leather.

> Police General Orders dated 24th April 1900 describe other items of uniform as follows:
>
> *Riding breeches: dark blue with oak-leaf stripes. Peaked Cap: with silver on the outside edge of the patent-leather peak; badge VR surmounted by a crown and*

wreath. Austrian Cap with silver tracing braid at top edges, the same badge as the peaked cap, centre of khaki colour.

The cloak and mackintosh are described as *ordinary military*.

Khaki undress is also described in this Order

NCOs of the Matabeleland Constabulary wore a blue tunic, braided across the chest in a lighter blue and with blue facings on the skirts of the tunic, but none on the collar. Their sleeves had pointed tracing braid with mohair braid at the edges. Rank badges appear to have been of white or metalled cloth upon a dark blue background. The Austrian Cap worn was of the same pattern as that for the Mashonaland Constabulary. The ensemble was completed with white *duck* trousers worn with black shoes or ankle boots. Constables wore the same uniform as sergeants (but with no braiding across the chest of the tunic) and a plain white *Universal* helmet worn in place of the Austrian Cap.

Officer's Cross or Shoulder Belt, Pouch and Fittings (MMP)

Title Brass – Matabeleland Native Police

Plate 8

Plate 9. The Matabeleland Native Police: 1893 – 1896

The Matabeleland Native Police (the first of Rhodesia's African Police to have the nickname of the *Black Watch* applied to them) was formed, at the same time as the Matabeleland Mounted Police, at the end of the year 1893. Raised as an armed force under the local command of Native Commissioners, many of their number were drawn from the two senior Ndebele regiments and included a nephew of Lobengula.

Besides ensuring that the orders of Native Commissioners were carried out, their purpose was to maintain communication and provide a better understanding between the two races. Unfortunately, as is often the case, a little power corrupted and by their high-handed treatment of their compatriots more fuel was added to the flames which fanned into the Matabele rebellion.

On the outbreak of the rebellion, a large number of the Native Police were loyal and may well have remained so. However, many had gone over to the insurgents taking their arms with them and the loyalty of others was doubtful. The corps was therefore disbanded.

The Matabeleland Native Police were given the minimum of uniform. The individual constable, however, considered that he had been given incalculable riches, providing an enormous boost to his prestige among his fellows. The uniform consisted of a blue dungaree tunic worn over calf-length shorts or trousers of the same material or, more usually, those of khaki drill material. Tunic and trousers were held by a coarse canvas belt. The wearing of a blue-coloured fez or a blue field service cap similar to that worn by the Matabeleland Mounted Police (but with no distinguishing badge) appeared optional. Towards the end of the life of this unit the title *MNP* was worn on the stand-up collar of the tunic.

Each man was issued with a Martini-Henry rifle, a bandolier with 40 rounds of ammunition and a long bayonet.

Sergeant – Matabeleland Constabulary

Plate 9

THE JAMESON RAID had deprived the country of the greater part of its only organized and disciplined fighting force, leaving areas of settlement largely unprotected. The ending of the raid in defeat, albeit at the hands of his own kind, proved a blow to the prestige of the white man in the eyes of the African. Plagues of locusts, drought and outbreaks of rinderpest that had occurred since the coming of the European, were evils ascribed to his influence. The confiscation of cattle as a result of the Matabele War, the effect of labour regulations upon one of the world's most indolent peoples, the tactless and sometimes oppressive conduct of Native Police, the curtailment of raiding, but most of all the loss of their independence, were enough to prove to the Ndebele that civilization, in this form certainly, was a burden that they could well do without.

As a result of the death of their king, Lobengula, no strong leader was on hand to guide the destinies of a discontented people. The power of the witchdoctors, however, had not declined. It was they who incited the tribes to revolt. The rebellion soon spread to Mashonaland. In the case of the Shona, it was not so much discontent—although they too disliked the labour regulations—as opportunism and the influence of two witchdoctors, Kaguli and Nyanda.

Isolated settlers were massacred and homesteads pillaged and burned. Where possible, small communities were gathered into laagers and defended. As many people as possible were drawn into the larger centres, as was done in the case of Inspector Nesbitt's heroic patrol to Mazoe. Once more it was the police, despite their reduced number, that formed the nucleus of the forces operating against the rebels, and once again the settlers rallied to form volunteer units as they had done in the Matabele War.

The final subjugation of the Ndebele was completed by August 1896 with a series of *Indabas* held by Cecil Rhodes with the Chiefs and Indunas of the nation, deep in the fastness of the Matopos hills.

Surprisingly, it was the Shona (not notably a warrior-race) who took longer to subdue, and they continued to threaten peace for some months thereafter. However, a decisive police action at Matshayongombi's kraal, in the district east of Salisbury on 24th July 1896, effectively broke the back of the rebellion that petered out by October. During the rebellion 32 policemen were either killed in action or died as a result of wounds; eight others were severely wounded.

At the outset, the police contribution to the defence of the country was negligible because of Jameson's adventure to the south. By the time the campaigns had ended, however, the BSAP was the only military force left in the field. Afterwards, it was entirely responsible for the maintenance of peace and good order in Rhodesia.

Plate 10. The Volunteers: 1896 – 1897

As the rebellion in Matabeleland spread to Mashonaland, the small number of police remaining as a result of the Jameson Raid were hard pressed to hold the line. Settlers again rallied to form volunteer units as they had done in the Matabele War. The Rhodesia Horse Volunteers, the Bulawayo Field Force, Beal's Column, the Burgher Force, the Umtali Rifles and Umtali Artillery and Honey's Scouts were but a few of the units formed in 1896. Imperial troops, represented in the Mashonaland Field Force, the Natal Troop and men returning from the Jameson Raid became progressively involved as time went by. It was, nevertheless, the volunteers who deserve most of the credit for finally quelling the rebellion in 1897.

Just as in the Matabele War three years earlier, the volunteer, on joining, donned whatever uniforms was available to him. Many men turned out in kit that they had worn in the Company's Police or in the Pioneers. In the main, however, outfits were very much the same as the Trooper's uniform of 1890 and included, on occasions, items of civilian clothing (for example the contemporary Norfolk Jacket) adapted as uniform.

While the polka dot or *guinea fowl* pattern puggaree was adopted by a number of units, it seems clear that it was regulation wear for the Mashonaland Field Force. Other favoured puggarees were of white or khaki cotton material, probably because this was the more readily available and suitable soft cloth.

The Maxim machine gun was a weapon that the early Rhodesians seized upon eagerly. As was to be proved in later wars, it was the great leveller when the many were arrayed against the few. This was the original belt-fed machine gun of .45 inch calibre using Martini-Henry ammunition that was later redesigned to accept the .303 inch bullet. Although the Maxim was adopted by the British Army in 1891, it was not used extensively on campaign until it was proved a success in the Matabele War. In fact, the first unit to bring the gun into action was the Bechuanaland Border Police under Colonel Gould-Adams. It appears also that it was a Rhodesian innovation to mount a Maxim upon high two-wheeled carriages drawn by a pair of horses. This gave the weapon mobility and had the effect of raising the operator's head some five feet above the ground while affording cover behind an armoured shield.

Plate 10

Plate 11. Rhodesia Horse Volunteers: 1896 – 1902

Strictly speaking the Rhodesia Horse belongs in the family tree of the Rhodesian Army, in particular to that of the Royal Rhodesia Regiment. However, no apology is offered for including it in this account, as the Rhodesia Horse was also one of the first volunteer regiments that were called upon to assist the early police in times of emergency, in much the same was as the BSA Police Reserve, in its various forms, did later.

The Rhodesia Horse Volunteers were raised in Mashonaland in April 1896 for service against rebels in Matabeleland. Initially comprising an Artillery Troop, a Mounted Troop and a Dismounted Troop, the Horse increased in size to two (Eastern and Western) divisions distributed in Salisbury, Umtali, Victoria and Bulawayo.

As successors to the Mashonaland and Salisbury Horse, the regiment served throughout the rebellion amalgamating with the Burgher Force to form the Salisbury Field Force in June 1896. Nevertheless, the Rhodesia Horse managed to retain its unit identity and had the honour of representing the volunteers on the occasion of Queen Victoria's Jubilee celebrations in June 1897. This notwithstanding the fact that BSAP Regimental Orders dated 31st March 1897 record: *The Mounted Troop, Rhodesia Horse Volunteers (and Victoria Rifles) arrived in Salisbury for disbandment this day.*

The Rhodesia Regiment was formed by Colonel Plumer in August 1899 for service in the Boer War. Surprisingly, despite the regimental title, the majority of the 450 men of its establishment were recruited from the Cape Province; but one squadron—*E*—was reserved entirely for Rhodesians and which, using British Army nomenclature of the era, might be referred to as E (Rhodesia Horse) Squadron, Rhodesia Regiment. At the end of the Boer War the Rhodesian Horse, like the old soldier, seemed to fade away as an identifiable unit being absorbed completely into the Rhodesia Regiment.

As a volunteer unit, the Rhodesia Horse must have gone through the same vagaries of dress as did other early corps. The uniform illustrated is that worn for the Diamond Jubilee celebration. The tunic and breeches were khaki either of cotton or twill cloth; certainly a finer material than drill was utilized if the interpretation of photographic record is correct. The dark brown felt hat was turned up at the left side and secured to a red puggaree with the regimental badge. The badge, like that of the parent Company's police, was of cloth, woven red upon blue, depicting the lion and tusk surrounded by the title: *Rhodesia Horse—BSAC*. Other items of the uniform include dark blue puttees, black ankle boots, jack spurs and chains, black Sam Browne belt and revolver holster with a khaki lanyard secured about the collar. The bandolier was usually of brown leather.

The Rhodesia Horse were the first of the British South Africa Company's forces to adopt the lance for ceremonial purposes, when these were carried by the Diamond Jubilee Troop in 1897. The Queen Victoria Museum in Harare, Zimbabwe, had at one time two such lances bearing the Company's pennant. These were located in the Cathedral Hotel, Salisbury, in Wiltshire, England in 1963. It is interesting to speculate how they arrived in that location. Perhaps the model for the adjoining illustration could have supplied the answer. The original photograph caught our trooper very much in a *morning after the night before* pose and in a uniform that may well have been slept in. Another photograph of this same trooper, clearly taken earlier, shows him immaculately turned out *On Parade*, carrying a lance, and mounted on a magnificent black steed.

Cap Badge – Rhodesia Horse

R.HAMLEY '99

Plate 11

A FURTHER RESULT of the Jameson Raid was that the early Rhodesian Police forces were removed from the authority of the Chartered Company and placed under the direct control of the United Kingdom High Commissioner in South Africa. On 1st October 1896, while still on active duty engaged in suppressing the rebellion, the Mashonaland and the Matabeleland Mounted Police were integrated to form the *Rhodesian Mounted Police*. This title was not retained for long, however, for in General Orders dated 29th December 1896, the Commandant-General laid down a fixed establishment for "... the Mashonaland and Matabeleland divisions of the *British South Africa Police*".

The "fixed establishments", incidentally, were based upon the structure of a British cavalry regiment and included an artillery troop to form part of the Depot Troop, and a mule battery for the Matabeleland Division. The Mule Battery consisted of a number of two and a half inch rifle-barrelled, muzzle-loading, mountain screw guns, that had an interesting history of their own:

Originally these weapons had been the property of the 10th Mountain Battery of the Indian Army, brought over to Natal in 1880 and captured by the Boers at Majuba Hill in 1881. Subsequently recaptured by the British, they had found their way to Rhodesia, most likely with the Mashonaland Field Force.

Police General Orders dated 22nd August 1898 formally recorded the change of title to the British South Africa Police:

> *His Excellency the High Commissioner's Police Notice No. 18 of 1897 is published for general information:*
>
> *It is hereby notified for public information that the white Police Forces serving within the limits of the Bechuanaland Protectorate and the British South Africa Company's territories will in future be designated "The British South Africa Police" and will be composed of four divisions as follows:*
>
> 1. *Bechuanaland Protectorate Division*
> 2. *Matabeleland Division*
> 3. *Mashonaland Division*
> 4. *North Zambezi Division*
>
> *The Native Police in the Bechuanaland Protectorate will continue to be styled "The Protectorate Native Police"*

MANY AND VARIED were the duties and the exploits of the BSAP during this time. Exploits that warrant several chapters in a more formal history beyond the scope of this present work. It is enough to mention, however, that together with the Rhodesia Regiment, portions of both the Mashonaland and Matabeleland Divisions of the Force, stationed at Fort Tuli, prevented the invasion of Rhodesia by Boer forces under Sarel Eloff (a nephew of President Kruger) and the German Von Dalwig. Men of the Bechuanaland Division provided the fighting crews for the armoured trains and served the guns in Mafeking. Members of the BSAP, therefore, were present as part of both the besieged and the relieving forces of this famous little town. After the relief of Mafeking in May 1900, the BSAP provided troops for the long drawn-out campaign against the Boers in the Western Transvaal. They were finally released for return to Rhodesia when the South African War ended in May 1902.

It was a hallowed tradition in the Force that King Edward VII had been pleased to mark his appreciation of the services of the BSAP in the Boer War by conferring upon the Corps the status of a Regiment and by the presentation to it of a Regimental Colour. The Colour was presented by Lord Milner at Mafeking on 5th October 1904, and for many years afterward it was afforded all honours due to such regimental icon. However when, because of its dilapidated state, a replacement was sought prior to the 1937 Coronation, in the resulting negotiations the Army Council ruled: *...the flag presented to the British South Africa Police in 1904 was a banner.*[2] It was not, after all, a Colour. Deeply offended, the BSAP tended to regard this as but another example of *perfidious Albion*. (Nevertheless, it was as a Colour or Standard that the Banner was last paraded—in review before Her Majesty the Queen Mother—in Salisbury on 30th May 1960. Thereafter, until the regiment's demise in 1980, it was lodged in a place of honour in the Officers' Mess in the Police Depot).

---

2 Vide—William Gale *Rhodesia's Most Exclusive Club* in *Rhodesian Scene*—1973

British South Africa Police Dispatch Rider (Salisbury to Marandellas) 1900

AT THE CONCLUSION of the South African War the Force again suffered under the economic axe and was obliged to reorganize. The short-lived North Zambezi Division had disappeared in June 1898, merging with the Mashonaland Division upon the formation of the Barotseland Native Police when Northern Rhodesia became a separate entity.

BSA Police General Orders of 5th March 1903 recorded:

> *... the Bechuanaland Division of the British South Africa Police and the Protectorate Native Police no longer exist. The Police Force of the Bechuanaland Protectorate will in future be known as the Bechuanaland Protectorate Police.*

The remaining divisions were amalgamated into one composite force under the command of Lieutenant-Colonel William Bodle, DSO who had been the first man enlisted in the old Company's Police.

The Commandant-General's Orders of 5th October 1903 read:

> *The duties of the BSA Police combine those of a military force for the defence of (Southern) Rhodesia and those of a police force for the preservation of peace, prevention of crime and the apprehension of offenders. As the latter duties naturally predominate in peacetime it is necessary for the Force to be broken up into detachments for the more effective policing of the Colony.*

Pursuant to these instructions eleven troops were established—five each in Mashonaland and Matabeleland and one in reserve in the Depot. Each troop was a complete and separate unit under the command of an officer holding the rank of an inspector.

Two ceremonial occasions of note that occurred during this period were the funeral of Cecil Rhodes and the Coronation of King Edward VII. Cecil John Rhodes died at Muizenburg in the Cape Province on 26th March 1902. At his request, the man who had made the land his own, and who was unquestionably its founder and hero, was buried in Rhodesia. It was fitting that it should be men of the police force that he had created, who escorted his body to its last resting-place at *World's View* in the Matopos Hills.

Queen Victoria died in 1901 and at the coronation of her successor, a BSA Police contingent consisting of one officer and 12 other ranks were commended for their *smartness, soldierly bearing and good behaviour*.

In February 1909, control of the BSAP reverted to the Company's administration, with the proviso that the Force be restrained from undertaking any military enterprise unless declared (by the United Kingdom Government) to be *on active service*. The, until then, independently administered BSA Police and the Southern Rhodesian Constabulary were formally amalgamated on 1st December 1909, the latter to become the Foot Branch or *Town Police* of the Force.

Plate 12. The British South Africa Police: Trooper 1903

The non-native or "white" police forces serving within the limits of the Bechuanaland Protectorate and the British South Africa Company's territories were merged to become the British South Africa Police in December 1896. The Native Police in the Bechuanaland Protectorate continued to be styled *The Protectorate Native Police*. The BSA Company's Native Police had been disbanded at the onset of the rebellion, although there is little doubt that many of their number had their services retained by magistrates and Native Commissioners—subsequently to form the nucleus of the Native Messenger Corps.

The reorganization of the combined police forces commenced with the conclusion of the Matabele Rebellion. At four *indabas* held in the Matopos hills in August, September and October 1896, Cecil Rhodes had talked peace to the Ndebele. The Mashona were more intractable, finally surrendering to the inevitable in October 1897. Imperial troops then withdrew and local military forces were stood down. To the newly reconstituted police force was left the task of mopping up, collecting guns and other weapons and restoring order generally.

For administrative purposes, the country was divided into districts, each under a tribal headman. Small units of police garrisoned outstations in support of Native Commissioners. Larger headquarter stations were established as new townships came into being.

While the British South Africa Company paid for and maintained the police force, its operations were strictly controlled by the British Government in the person of the High Commissioner.

While it had started life with four divisions, the British South Africa Police underwent continuing rationalization, firstly by the merging of the North Zambezi Division with the Mashonaland Division when Northern Rhodesia became a separate entity, and again when the Bechuanaland Division was disbanded in 1903. During this period and within its remaining divisions the BSAP continued to function primarily as sub-units of Mounted or District Police and of Foot or Town Police (Constabulary).

Police General Orders dated 23rd September 1899 record that NCOs and men of the British South Africa Police received an issue of blue serge tunic and overalls and a khaki tunic and slacks. Knee boots and a grey tunic were a biannual issue. The trooper illustrated is wearing full dress then known as *Full Blues*. At first a BBP pattern felt hat with the old pattern green puggaree was issued. Then a grey felt hat (with brown puggaree), worn turned up at the left side and pinned with the regimental badge, was introduced in 1897. Members of the Artillery Troop, who considered themselves the *elite* of the Corps, wore red bands around the tops of their puggaree. The full dress tunic was of blue serge with regimental badges at the collar and BSAP insignia in brass on the shoulder straps. Breeches were dark brown, often near wine-coloured, with white strapping that was heavily blancoed for parades. Dark blue puttees had replaced knee boots in 1899 and were worn with black ankle (Southall) boots and jack spurs. There was no belt to this uniform but a white dispatch case with shoulder strap, rather in the fashion of a sash, was worn on most ceremonial occasions—although there is no record that this was sanctioned by orders.

When ordered to bear arms, the Trooper illustrated would have had with him a Magazine Lee-Enfield or Lee-Metford rifle. These were replaced by the SMLE rifle in 1909. His brown leather bandolier was converted to hold .303 inch ammunition. This item too, was replaced a short time later by the mounted infantry bandolier introduced during the Boer war. The saddle was of ordinary hunting pattern with *Dees* for a patrol tin, blanket, saddlebags and rifle bucket. The rifle bucket of the period was a rather unsatisfactory item of equipment known as the *Namaqua* pattern bucket.

The mule battery attached to the Matabeleland Division consisted of two 2.5 inch, rifled, muzzle-loading mountain screw guns of some 400lbs. These guns had an interesting history of their own. They were originally the property of the 10th Mountain battery of the Indian Army, brought over to Natal in 1880 and captured by the Boers at the battle of Majuba Hill in 1881. Subsequently recaptured by the British they found their way to Rhodesia, probably with the Mashonaland Field Force.

This type of mountain gun had been introduced into the British Army in 1879 and was not replaced by the 10-pounder breech-loading mountain gun until 1896. It was most likely at the time when muzzle-loaders were being replaced by the breech-loading weapon, that these particular guns were made available to the British South Africa Police.

RML Mountain Guns were compact, solid pieces of ordnance that were readily dismantled for conveyance by mules on their specially designed packsaddles. It required five mules to carry a complete gun—plus 20 rounds of ammunition. It is thought that the mules had come from the British Army with the guns, as all were at least 18 years of age.

Men for the Artillery Troop were selected for their strength and physical fitness and took great pride in the speed and precision with which they could assemble a gun and bring it into action.

Plate 12

Plate 13. The BSA Police: Native Constable 1898 – 1905

Upon the amalgamation of the Rhodesian police forces and the formation of the British South Africa Police in 1896, a Native contingent of 300 men was authorized. At the time there was, understandably, a reluctance to recruit local Africans because of experiences suffered in the rebellion. Initially, therefore, use was made of *Cape Boys*, Bechuanas and some Zulus, all foreign Africans with no tribal affinity to the indigenous Rhodesian.

In 1898 a Reserve Company of 150 aliens (Angoni) was recruited as Native Police, to be trained as part of a military force to protect the early settlers in the event of further rebellion. The Reserve Company became the Mashonaland Native Police in 1899, but recruitment was still restricted to Angonis who served on a month to month basis.

Local Africans were not recruited into the police until the establishment of the District Native Police early in 1903 when a force of 450 Southern Rhodesian natives was raised. They were instructed as District Police and carried firearms only when under the command of a European and were engaged upon duties that required the use of arms. At all other times they carried the native knobkerrie or fighting stick. In December 1903 the District Native Police became the BSA Native Police with men of the Mashonaland Native Police and Native Messengers being permitted to re-engage into the new force.

District Native Police Muleteer 1903

At the time illustrated (about 1900) the following clothing was issued: one suit of khaki tunic and knickers, one blue frock and one pair of blue knickers, two pairs of puttees (not often worn), two caps or fezzes and a greatcoat. Brass buttons peculiar to the Native Police were worn and the regimental title, utilized in place of a badge, pinned down the red cord tassel of the fez. The Martini-Henry rifle and bandolier were issued only for armed duties.

Police Headquarters Circular No 14 of January 1905 had this to say with regard to Native Police clothing:

> *To ensure uniformity amongst the BSAP Native Police, the following regulations for wearing the new pattern uniform are issued:*
>
> *Blue Serge Jumper: To be worn on patrols, fatigues and night guards.*
>
> *Blue Dungaree Tunics: To be worn only on parade and in townships, walking out, etc.*
>
> *Fez: To be worn on the right side of the head with the tassel over the right ear; the crown of the Fez to be unfolded.*
>
> *Khaki knickers: To be fitted so that they reach no lower than the knee.*

Plate 13

Plate 14. The British South Africa Police: Officers 1907

Police General Order No 179 dated 3rd February 1902 records—*The following is the authorized dress for officers:*

Full Dress:

1. Blue serge coat (Gilt badges and plain buttons); 2. White breeches; 3. Blue puttees; 4. Black ankle boots; 5. Spurs and chains (swan-neck pattern); 6. Felt hat, puggaree and chinstrap—regimental badge; 7. Brown Sam Browne belt and revolver with white lanyard; 8. Gauntlets—white buckskin.

Undress: For drill or marching order, parades, garrison duties, etc.

1. Khaki serge coat—gilt badges and buttons; 2. Khaki cord breeches; 3. Khaki puttees; 4. Felt hat and puggaree; 5. Brown ankle boots; 6. Spurs and chains; 7. Sam Browne belt; 8. Brown doeskin gloves.

The following may be worn for dismounted duty under arms:

1. Khaki overalls; 2. Wellington boots; 3. Staff pattern cap khaki; 4. Khaki field service cap.

Mess Dress:

1. Blue serge jacket, roll collar, gilt badges and buttons; 2. White linen collar, black silk tie; 3. Blue serge overalls with 1½ in. braid (oak-leaf); 4. Field service cap, all blue, fine gold piping.

Pouch Plate with British South Africa Police Cypher

In June 1903 the military titles of commissioned rank in the BSAP were dropped in official communications—although they continued to be used in other circumstances.

Police General Order No 393 of 2nd October 1903 states:

> *In future the following badges of rank will be worn by officers upon their shoulder straps:*
>
> *Commandant: Crown and Star*
> *Chief Inspector: Crown*
> *Inspector: Three Stars*
> *Sub-Inspector: Two Stars*
> *Acting Sub-Inspector: One Star*

Dress Circular No 92 dated 29th August 1907 states:

Sword:	*Cavalry pattern blade with pierced white metal hilt. Pommel and back of hand plain—silver or nickel-plated to individual taste.*
Scabbard:	*White metal with two rings—silver or nickel-plated to individual taste.*
Sword Knot:	*Brown plaited leather with white buff acorn.*
Sword Belt:	*Blue webbing 2¼ in. wide with white web suspender, brown leather sword slings and billets and white metal billet buckles.*
Pouch Belt:	*Brown bridle leather 2½ in. wide fitted with studs at end to attach pouch.*
Furniture in front of belt:	*Whistle fitted onto a plate and three chains connected to a chain plate. The whole of Corps pattern and silver-plated in white metal.*
Pouch:	*Brown leather fitted with a white metal plate to front of flap. Plate fitted with BSAP cypher and crown in gilt metal. Pouch fitted with white metal furniture to attach to pouch belt. Flap of pouch and furniture silver-plated.*
Sam Browne Belt:	*Revolver lanyard now approved.*
Whistle and Lanyard:	*Attach to shoulder brace.*

Helmet Badge – Southern Rhodesia Constabulary

Plate 14

Plate 15. The Town Police: Constable 1909 – 1918

In 1903 the Matabeleland Constabulary was amalgamated with the Mashonaland Constabulary to form the Southern Rhodesia Constabulary (SRC). To begin with the SRC was independent of the BSAP, but gradually the two were merged into one organization.

Approval for the transfer of the SRC from the control of the United Kingdom High Commissioner to that of the British South Africa Company was given later the same year. It was not regularized by proclamation, however, until 1904. Police General Order No 516 dated 13th May 1904 notes the proclamation being given effect by a formal hand-over to the Administrator by the *Commandant General responsible for all Police and Military Forces in Rhodesia*. Following a ceremony at the SRC's Kopje Police Station, Chief Inspector (Local Major) Drury, a BSAP veteran of the Jameson Raid, assumed command of the Southern Rhodesia Constabulary. His predecessor, Chief Inspector Fuller, became the Chief Staff Officer of the BSAP. Fuller, later succeeded Colonel Bodle when that officer retired in 1909, at which time Drury returned to the SRC as Chief Staff Officer. Later, Drury was to return to the BSA Police to succeed Fuller, as Commandant, in 1911.

In February 1909 control of the BSAP was transferred from the Imperial Government to the Company's administration—with the proviso, however, that the Force was debarred from undertaking any military enterprise unless declared to be *on active service* by the United Kingdom Government. Now independent both the BSAP and the SRC were formally amalgamated on 1st December 1909—at which time the *professionals* of the Constabulary suffered a marked cut in pay in order to bring their salaries into line with those of the BSA Police.

With the amalgamation, the Southern Rhodesia Constabulary became the Foot Branch or Town Police of the Force.

Dating from the days of the old Mashonaland and Matabeleland Constabulary and the Mounted Police of the BSA Company, there had always been a robust rivalry between the Constable and the Trooper. Each would declare that he was the *real* policeman. The Trooper had the inherited superiority of the mounted man over the foot-slogger, and the Constable all the self-confidence of a man who stood upon his own two feet. In those days, Town police were selected for their stature and appearance and preference was given to men with previous police experience. Should a District policeman, seeking the advantages of comparative civilization, transfer to the Town Branch, he was obliged to serve for a period on probation.

It was from within the ranks of the Town Police that the specialized units of the Force were to be formed: the CID, the Staff Branch, Traffic and Dog Sections, to name but a few. It was these units that were to maintain inter-branch competitiveness in the years to come. The title *Trooper* was to be discontinued after the Second World War. Outside of the Depot and the combative Mounted Unit, the horse was to become redundant and the old rivals, the Town and District Branches, were to be united on a common roll in 1965.

A Constable of the period illustrated wore the following clothing and equipment:

Blue serge tunic and trousers, the latter without straps. Corps pattern black boots without spurs. A white helmet with white cotton puggaree by day and a blue forage cap, if required, by night. The white helmet was peculiar to the Town Branch of the Force. Other items worn were the whistle and chain secured at the top button of the tunic and held in the left breast pocket. The armband, the sign of a man on duty, was adopted from the British Police Forces but was discontinued in 1930. No waist belt was worn with this dress order.

A man on probation for transfer from the mounted to the foot branch of the Force would wear khaki frock and trousers, corps pattern black boots, khaki helmet, whistle and chain and the armband described. Bandoliers were not worn at any time on Town duty during this period, except when men were specifically ordered out under arms.

Dress circular No 19 dated 14th March 1910 states:

NCOs and men employed on town police duties at stations where white helmets are provided will not wear waist belts or armlets.

Dress circular No 32 of 19th April 1910 records:

All NCOs and men on Town Duty should wear numerals... in khaki tunics the numerals will be worn where the collar badge is placed on blue tunics. In blue tunics the numerals will be placed half an inch behind the collar badge.

Town Police: Collar Badge & Numerals

Plate 15

IN THE GREAT War of 1914 – 1918, as in the Second World War, no other colony or territory in the British Empire donated so large a proportion of its available manpower to the cause of freedom, as did the infant colony of Rhodesia. That Rhodesia was able to do this was largely due to the BSAP. In 1914 the only body of men ready and trained for war—and fit and keen to fight on any front—was the police.

Naturally it was their expectation to be first into the fight. It was not to be, however, for the Force was ordered to *stand-fast* for the duration. Bitterly disappointed, the would-be warriors had to allow civilians to go to war.

To quote from Lieutenant-Colonel A.E. Capell's book *The Second Rhodesia Regiment at War*:

> *Called out on active service they stand undecorated, for no medal comes their way, but an unstinted deed of honour is their due for they permitted, sanctioned and guaranteed the exodus and fully redeemed the unspoken pledge. Cede ye them the right of the line, as a tribute to worth for value received.*

So great was the disappointment, that the odd deserter from the Force managed to find his way into the trenches in Flanders. Others, with recent army service, managed by devious means to obtain their release and to rejoin their former regiments. What opportunities came their way were eagerly pursued. Volunteers, however, always exceeded the numbers required and strict selection had to be enforced.

No. 1 Mobile Troop was mobilized in August 1914. At Salisbury it entrained for Victoria Falls where it was joined by No. 4 Troop from Bulawayo, a Machine Gun Section from Depot and 40 armed Native Police, to form the *BSAP Mobile Column* under Major Capell, DSO. The Column, less No. 4 Troop which was recalled to Bulawayo, proceeded to Kazangula on the Zambezi River border between Rhodesia and Bechuanaland. From there it moved to Sesheke where it was joined by a column from Northern Rhodesia. The combined column then bore down upon the German fort at Schuckmansburg in German South West Africa. The Germans surrendered without a shot being fired. Additional Northern Rhodesia Police (NRP)arrived a month later and, as there were then sufficient Native Police to garrison the captured fort, the BSAP were withdrawn to Salisbury. A German flag, previously flown from the masthead at Fort Schuckmansburg, came out secreted under a trooper's shirt. Encased under glass, it could be viewed as a *Trophy of War* half a century or more afterward in the vestibule to the Sergeants' Mess in the BSA Police Depot.

Lacking recruits, the Police Depot in Salisbury turned energetically to the training of the Southern Rhodesia Volunteers, the Rhodesia Regiment and to the formation of the Rhodesia Native Regiment (later the Rhodesian African Rifles [RAR]), for which the Force provided many of its officers and NCOs.

In 1915 an opportunity for active war service came with the formation of the Southern Rhodesia Column, known also as the BSAP Service Column or, acknowledging the skill and daring of its commander, *Murray's Column*. After securing the Northern Rhodesia border, Murray's column marched into German East Africa as part of

Brigadier General Northey's *Norforce*, where it was engaged in continuous operations against the German General von Lettow-Vorbeck until 1918. Contact with the enemy was continuous, at times culminating in decisive actions—one in particular where the BSAP distinguished itself in a bayonet-charge against a heavily defended position. The area of operations was vast and it is calculated that well over 10,000 miles were marched. Natural obstacles were enormous and a lack of transport and difficulties with communications added to the stress of combat. Perhaps the greatest hazard other than enemy action, however, was fever and dysentery that took a terrific toll—so much so that a fit man was worth his weight in gold.

Murray's *ubiquitous and gallant Rhodesians* earned high praise and brought further laurels to their country's name. The second VC to be awarded to a member of the Force (the first going to Inspector R. C. Nesbitt of Mazoe Patrol fame) was won in this campaign by Sergeant (later Captain) F. C. Booth, for bravery in action and for rallying disorganized native troops. Sergeant Booth had already won the DCM and had been mentioned in despatches.

For police remaining in Rhodesia life was much more mundane, consisting of day-to-day policing and patrolling, enlivened on occasions—more often than not as a result of false or exaggerated reports—by patrols in strength under mobilization conditions.

The BSAP ended the war as it began, as Rhodesia's first line of defence. In the years to follow it was to learn, as Peter Gibbs[3] says: ...*the need to shed the image and trappings of one of Queen Victoria's mounted infantry regiments—and while still preserving its regimental dignity—to establish public respect for its reputation as an efficient police force.*

3 Peter Gibbs: *The Right of the Line.* Kingstons Limited (Rhodesia) 1974.

Plate 16. The BSA Police Service Column: Trooper 1915

Whilst it must be accepted that in the field of operations, particularly in the arid East African climate, all but essential items of clothing and equipment would have been discarded, the Trooper illustrated is portrayed as wearing the Light Marching Order of 1915, much as he might have appeared when first mustered to the Police Depot.

Photographs taken at this time suggest that many of the helmets issued to other ranks were rounder and more like a civilian topee or pith hat than that shown, and were possibly of South African or Indian origin. The helmet depicted was an improved edition of the earlier Colonial and Wolseley Pattern Helmets, with a wider brim and projecting more in the front. The *Helmet Universal Colonial Pattern* came into general use after the South African War of 1899 – 1902. It is described in the clothing book as:

> *Helmet—Cork, covered with khaki (or white) cloth in six seams with buff leather at the bottom. Khaki covered zinc ventilator at the top. Green lining. Helmet worn with 3/8 in. wide curb-chain chinstrap and spike when worn for ceremonial.*

Chevrons indicating an NCO's rank were of khaki coloured tape. Puttees were dark brown and the boots of mounted infantry pattern. British Army 1908 pattern infantry equipment had been introduced and to this was added a cotton bandolier that held 50 rounds of .303 inch ammunition.

The SMLE rifle was first produced in 1902 and issued to the British Army in 1905. It was first issued to B, C, E, G and K troops of the BSAP in 1909 when the Magazine Lee Enfield was withdrawn. Designed originally as a mounted infantry weapon to replace the MLE and Lee Metford rifles, it was truly a masterpiece of its time. With an 18-inch long bayonet and in the hands of an infantryman in the *Queen of Battles*, it probably contributed more than any other weapon to winning the First World War. The SMLE had a long life and went through a number of marks. During the 1970s it could still be found with the BSAP on ceremonial parades.

A favourite weapon with the Corps at this time was the Lewis Machine Gun, a .303 inch light machine gun introduced in 1915 as an infantry support weapon. When received by the BSAP only a short time later, ingenious horse furniture was devised to convert it to a mounted infantry weapon. It too saw long service with the Force until replaced by the Bren Gun during World War II.

Rifle (SMLE) No 1, MkIII & Bayonet

Plate 16

THE YEARS BETWEEN the First and Second World Wars were a time of growth and consolidation both for the Force and for the colony of Southern Rhodesia. The tenor of the times was marred only by the Great Depression, a world-wide affliction that obliged the police, in common with other government servants, to accept a substantial cut in pay. In comparison, plagues of locusts, outbreaks of foot and mouth disease with their resulting cattle cordons, and the Rail Strike of 1929 were but minor irritations.

Over the years the white population of Rhodesia became increasingly disenchanted with government by the Chartered Company, and when the First World War was over, determined to rid themselves of its seemingly despotic rule. The Company too was having second thoughts as to the long-term profitability of its venture, and was only too pleased to rid itself of the uneconomic administrative role. Matters thus boiled down to a choice of two proposals: merger, as the fifth province of the Union of South Africa, or self-rule. After some lively political campaigning by the protagonists of both causes, Rhodesians opted for *Responsible Government*.

On the evening of 11th September 1923, the Company's flag flying at the masthead in the Police Depot, was hauled down for the last time. The next day Southern Rhodesia officially became a Self-Governing British Colony and a unique constitutional entity.

Corporal BSA Police 1928

Major General A.H.M Edwards, KBE, CB, retired from the BSAP on 31st January 1923 and, with his retirement, the rank of Commandant-General was discontinued. The senior serving officer of the Force from thenceforth was to be known as the Commissioner of Police. Control of the Force passed to the Attorney General and the Corps divided into three distinct branches: District Police, Town Police and the Criminal Investigation Department. Town and District Police were further sub-divided: District Police into Districts with headquarters at Salisbury, Umtali, Hartley, Victoria, Gwelo, Bulawayo and Gwanda. The Town Police co-existed at the same major centres. Whilst the rank of Trooper remained, the troop concept—the basic unit of a regiment of mounted infantry—as a system for administering the Force, was finally dead.

In 1924 Town Police units, other than those in Salisbury, were placed under the control of District Superintendents. The Railway Police, drawn from the Town Police and subsidiary to it, came into being with Rhodesia Railways paying for its upkeep. A Police Dog Section was formed but later fell into disuse, its potential not then recognized. The population of Rhodesia was growing steadily and with it the need for more extensive policing. Mobile columns were a feature of the era and mounted patrols showed the flag in the remotest areas of the country.

The period immediately prior to the Second World War was marked by an acceleration of development in Southern Rhodesia. The BSAP kept pace with the trend. The horse, originally representing the principal means of transportation, gave way rapidly to the motor cycle, the motor car and other forms of mechanization. Mounted Patrols began to be confined to the remoter parts of the Colony or to the special form of patrol where a horseman could be used to greater advantage.

In 1937 a mounted contingent of the BSAP represented Southern Rhodesia at the coronation of King George VI and, as was the case with the 1911 contingent before them, earned glowing praise for their immaculate turn-out and drill.

The importance and scope of the Criminal Investigation Department increased in parallel with the development of the country. In addition to the usual functions of CID, it administered Rhodesia's immigration laws, the senior officer of the department fulfilling the dual role of Chief Immigration Officer.

Times were changing. Leisurely patrols through the veldt on horse or by mule were being replaced by the only slightly less exhilarating rides through the bush on a PMC[4]. Modern police stations began to rise on the sites of formerly pole and daga hutted encampments. Fever-ridden outposts became a thing of the past. The BSAP had grown up, and the steady process of transition from a regiment of mounted infantry to an entirely civilian police force was almost, but not quite (and regrettably, as events were to prove, would never be), complete.

The last member to be appointed with the rank of Trooper was attested into the force on 2nd May 1949.

4 Prefacing a registration number to indicate—Police Motor Cycle.

Plate 17. The British South Africa Police: Sergeant (Riding Master) 1926

The end of the First World War saw the demise of *Full Blues*. Khaki Drill, originally the *fatigue dress, undress* or *drill order* of the Force became in various guises, all-purpose wear. Khaki, from the Urdu *Khak* meaning dust, was first introduced in India in the 1840s by Lumsden's Regiment of Guides and was adopted by the British Army during the Indian Mutiny. Many units dyed their white drill with palm juice, curry powder, coffee, etc., to obtain the desired effect. Generally it was agreed by commanders that whilst Khaki was practical, cool and comfortable, it was drab and not at all smart. As soon as the mutiny had ended, its use was forbidden. It did re-appear briefly as service dress in 1861 and again during the Second Afghan War of 1897, but was not recognized as *Foreign Service dress* until 1881. It took the Boer War to introduce it to South Africa as *General Service Dress* and it then found its way northward to the BSAP. With the regiment's reputation for smartness, it did not take the Police long to discover that a liberal application of starch improved its look considerably. Unfortunately, starch also made the material warm and uncomfortable to wear.

Sergeant – Ceremonial Colour Troop

The Helmet Universal (Colonial Pattern) was by this time on general issue. Helmets of this pattern were first approved for use by the Force on 7th March 1904 *...for patrol duties, but not with full dress or full dress tunics.* Chinstraps were then worn buckled up over the front peak, except on parades and drill when they were worn at the point of the chin. The puggaree was of khaki cotton. When khaki drill became the full dress of the Force the Helmet Universal was worn on all suitable occasions.

The 50-round capacity Lee Enfield bandolier was designed for the mounted infantryman of the Boer war and was issued to the BSAP in 1910. It has been described as "cumbersome, loose and uncomfortable when riding, and by no means ornamental". This latter observation is debatable, however, for a highly polished bandolier was truly a sight to behold. Use of the bandolier was run down in 1943 and it was withdrawn entirely in 1952.

Universal saddles with saddle wallets were introduced in 1926 and were still in use in the Police Depot in 1980 on ceremonial escort duties and occasionally with the Mounted Troop.

Plate 17

Plate 18. The British South Africa Police: Sergeant (Native Town Police) 1930

The BSA Native Police was established in December 1903. Prior to this, Africans attested into the Force were employed as little more than messengers, interpreters, orderlies, as government agents and as a reserve of military force, rather than as the fully trained policemen they were to become later.

Rhodesia was then a large territory, well populated by natives but as yet sparsely inhabited by Europeans. Police work, therefore, was attended by difficulties of an unusual nature. Two distinct racial groups, with different languages and customs, presented the police with many problems. Obviously a great deal of police work would involve the native peoples and so African and European policemen would have to cooperate closely together. Thus the native constable took a giant step forward towards the equal partnership that he would share in the years to come.

Native Police recruits were selected from among young men between the ages of 20 and 30 from all tribes and clans. They were attested either as Native District Constables, Native Town Constables, Mounted District Native Constables and as Native Detectives depending upon their height and other capabilities. Each man had to be of good character. He was also very carefully screened to determine whether he was physically and mentally sound and fit in all respects for police service. During their early service recruits were carefully watched and obvious misfits were removed. In this way the possibility of any future abuses of power was minimized.

Mounted District Native Constables, whose mounts were mules, were employed mainly on border control duties. This branch of the Native Police was disbanded in the early 1930s and its men assimilated into other branches of the Force.

The Native Sergeant illustrated is shown as wearing *Full Dress*.

Uniforms were issued to Native Police upon attestation and periodically throughout their service. They were expected to wear uniform at all times and whilst a native policeman might be required to carry out certain duties in plain clothes, permission had to be sought for civilian apparel to be worn when off duty.

The following were the dress orders of the period:

Full Dress:	*Khaki tunic, cap and shorts. Belt, bandolier (when parading under arms) and handcuffs. Worn on guards, parades, inspections, station duty, when attending court and orderly rooms.*
Patrol Order No 1:	*Tunic, cap, shorts, haversack, bandolier, belt handcuffs, rolled cloak or coat, and water bottle. This dress order was worn on escort duty, when travelling by rail on transfer, when proceeding to District Headquarters or to any township.*

Patrol Order No 2:	*Cap, jumper (khaki) or jersey (blue), khaki shorts, bandolier, belt and handcuffs. This dress order was worn when employed on ordinary patrol duty.*
Drill Order:	*Cap, jersey, shorts, bandolier and belt, plus rifle.*
Fatigue Dress:	*Cap without cover or the old style fez, shorts, jersey or jumper.*

In the 1930s Native police did not carry regulation batons or sjamboks but were allowed to carry sticks or kerries. Haversacks, when worn, were unrolled and carried over the right shoulder, the top of the haversack in line with the left elbow. Coats were rolled and worn over the right shoulder and fastened with a strap. When it was necessary to carry blankets, these too were rolled and carried over the shoulders—horse collar fashion. Boots (Brown AP) were on issue to the District Mounted Police and to the Askari, but they did not become a general issue to the Native Police until 1941.

The Cap (Askari) was introduced shortly after the First World War to replace the fez. It was patterned to the cap issued to the Rhodesia Native Regiment which was in turn based upon that worn by the German Askari in East Africa. The Askari cap was phased out in the mid-1940s when replaced by the Helmet (Shako) referred to later.

The ubiquitous *S* Clasp waist-belt is probably the one item of uniform to be worn continuously since the occupation. Replaced by the Belt Clasp (Sliding Buckle) for European other ranks in 1948 and phased-out for wear by African Police in the 1960s, it nevertheless could still be found thereafter worn by recruits in the Depot and by (uniformed) telephone attendants. It was issued yet again as part of the uniform for the *Specials* when this branch of the Force was re-activated in 1974.

Helmet Badge Brass 1937

Plate 18

Plate 19. The British South Africa Police: Trooper (District Police) 1938

In the late 1920s the inadequacies of khaki drill as full dress being apparent, the authorities set their minds to the production of a new full dress uniform for the European other ranks of the Force. Prior to the First World War, officers of the BSAP had worn khaki serge, initially as undress uniform with a stand-up collar, and later with the demise of full blues, as full dress with roll collars being introduced in 1913. A complementary uniform for the other ranks was therefore required.

The new uniform was produced in 1928. As a police uniform it was perhaps unique, but it properly portrayed the Corps' dual role as both police and mounted infantry and Rhodesia's first line of defence. To quote from the May 1928 edition of the regimental magazine, *The Outpost*:

> *On 30th April the Governor, Lieutenant-Colonel Sir John Robert Chancellor, GCMG, GCVO, DSO, RE, held a final inspection of the Depot at Salisbury. The occasion marked the inauguration of the new full dress uniform for the District Police, namely the gabardine tunics in place of the khaki…*

The particular shade of khaki-green used in the gaberdine material led to the uniform being referred to as *Greens,* a sobriquet that persisted to the end.

Town Police were issued with the tunic at the same time, to be worn in their case with gabardine trousers in place of the Bedford-cord pantaloons worn by the District men.

At this time both the Town and District police wore a khaki-coloured lanyard with this uniform. The helmet chain and spike were introduced at about the same time. Leggings, however, were not introduced until 1930, khaki puttees being worn instead.

Other items on the scale of issue for European police at this time were:

Boots brown AP and Mounted Service; Field Service Cap with khaki cover; a cavalry coat (in the process of being replaced by coats British-warm and waterproof); a felt hat (for stables); khaki drill trousers, tunic and knickers (shorts).

Sergeants Major were permitted to wear roll collar tunics, like those of officers in 1936 and, at their own expense, purchase officer's pattern khaki shirts and ties. Roll collar tunics for ranks below that of Sergeant major were not introduced until after the Second World War.

Bandolier Lee Enfield 50 Rounds

Plate 19

AS A RESULT of lessons learned in the Great War, plans for possible mobilization were put in hand early in 1930. It was logical that the BSAP, which represented the largest single body of men under arms, should be regarded as the base upon which planning for war was to be developed. In October 1936, the Commissioner of Police assumed the title of *Commandant-General of Southern Rhodesia Forces* and it was thus that upon Colonel T. S. Morris, CBE fell the main burden of defence preparations.

At the outbreak of war, therefore, the police were ready to act immediately. Efficient groundwork prepared by the Security Branch for example, facilitated the early registration and internment of enemy aliens. The Force was declared to be on active service immediately upon the declaration of war and at once stood guard at the more important strategic points within and to the north of Southern Rhodesian territory. On 3rd September 1939, as Britain went to war with Germany, a patrol comprising European police and members of the Native Police Platoon from the Depot who had been guarding the Victoria Falls bridge, slipped into the Caprivi Strip to make the first active patrol of the war.

Their first duty being the defence of Rhodesia, the BSAP were again obliged to stand fast while their civilian contemporaries went early to the theatres of war. In so doing they relieved a considerable number of troops for service on the northern frontier of Kenya and for subsequent campaigns against the Italians in Somaliland.

The Depot once again came to the fore in the training of Rhodesian military units. The Light Battery, the Signal Company, the Mechanical Transport Company and the Internment Camp Corps received their basic training at the hands of police instructors.

Members of the BSAP formed the nucleus of the Rhodesian African Rifles. Twenty-nine European and 30 African policemen were drafted to the RAR to assist in its formation and training. The greater number remained with that regiment for the duration, whilst others left to join forces overseas and those of the Union of South Africa.

At the outbreak of war, indeed well before the war was declared, Police Headquarters in Salisbury was inundated with a flood of requests from members of the Force asking to be released for active service. The spate of requests reached such proportions that the authorities were obliged to issue Regimental Order 514 of 1940, instructing members to desist as they were *clogging up channels* with their applications. A comprehensive list of those whose qualifications made them suitable for secondment, was drawn up. It was from this number that members of the Force were detached for service in North Africa, where experienced personnel were required to create new police forces in areas formerly occupied by the enemy. They formed an important part of the British Military Administration, Middle East Forces.

Many arrived in areas where operations against the enemy were still proceeding. Their duties were carried out under trying and difficult circumstances in countries still occupied by enemy nationals and where the indigenous population were often non-responsive, if not openly hostile. Members of the BSAP served with great credit in many roles ranging from Civil Affairs Officers, recruiting and forming police forces in areas ravaged by occupation, to the control of border skirmishing, and participation in commando units and other raiding forces. They were to be found throughout Africa and beyond in units such as the Eritrean Police, the Eritrean Frontier Striking Force, the Tripolitania Police and the Cyrenaica Defence Force Gendarmerie. They served in Somalia, the Gold Coast, Abyssinia, the Sudan, Cyprus, the Aegean Islands and throughout the Middle East.

A high ranking British officer wrote to the then Commissioner of Police: *We can get men from elsewhere, but they have not the same experience and qualifications as do yours, who in addition to being very efficient police, have a good knowledge of military matters. We would be glad to take as many as you can send us.*

A number of members were killed in action and others taken prisoners of war. The greater proportion of those who left Rhodesia with the war rank of British Inspectors gained commissions in the forces to which they were attached. All who left the country made a name for themselves and upheld the traditions of the Force, as did their comrades who, much under strength, remained behind to police Rhodesia efficiently throughout the war.

Plate 20. The British South Africa Police: Corporal (Mobilization Order) 1939

BSA Police Standing Orders for 1939 – 40 set out mobilization dress orders for officers, warrant officers, sergeants, corporals and troopers for Mounted, Dismounted, Motor Cycle and Pedal Cycle duties. Fully accoutred in accordance with any of these, the effect upon man, horse and machine must have been reminiscent of the proverbial Christmas tree.

This illustration is based upon one of a series of very fine line drawings that appeared with those orders.

In Mobilization Order (Motor Cycle), officers were to be equipped as follows:

> *Field service cap with neck flap and goggles, khaki-drill tunic and knickers (shorts), a khaki shirt, vest and socks. Around the neck identification discs worn next to the skin. A revolver carried in a case or holster. An S Belt worn with shoulder brace. A lanyard and pouch containing 12 rounds of ammunition. Over the left shoulder a haversack containing a holdall, laces, a hairbrush, towel, soap, brass brush, a plate, mug and rations. Over the right shoulder a filled water bottle. Leggings, boots MS and gauntlets completed the ensemble.*

The following items were carried on the motor cycle:

Two blankets held with straps, a British-warm greatcoat, a shirt, khaki drill trousers and a spare pair of socks all wrapped in a reversed waterproof sheet. In addition, a mess tin, iron rations and two gallons of petrol.

Mobilization Order (Mounted) 1938

Plate 20

Plate 21. The British South Africa Police: British Inspector (Overseas) 1941

The uniform illustrated is that of a member of the BSA Police who is about to leave the Police Depot on secondment to North Africa as a British Inspector.

The open-necked bush-shirt was introduced in 1937 and intended for wear when patrolling hot areas such as the Zambezi Valley. However, this was the first time that it was used for the more formal occasion. As such it was welcomed for its comfort and coolness; certainly it was the envy of others in the embarkation camps in South Africa who were obliged to wear khaki serge battle dress.

The helmet worn was the standard *Universal* pattern. In this instance, the khaki-drill bush shirt was worn with a khaki shirt, khaki-coloured tie and lanyard and khaki-drill shorts of Indian Army pattern. Brown boots, leggings and the ubiquitous *S* belt were standard issue. The button-head swagger stick was an occasional affectation. Webbing haversacks and water-bottle carriers, worn over the right and left shoulders respectively, hung level with the waist belt. A field service cap was issued which in a dark (Police) blue with gold piping was reminiscent of that worn by NCOs of the Force at the turn of the century.

Once serving with the units to which they were attached, members adopted the uniform of the foster-regiment, but retained their own regimental badges.

Badge, British Inspector, Slip–on

Plate 21

THE SECOND WORLD WAR temporarily put an end to recruiting for the BSAP. Although many of those who had served outside the Colony returned to normal duties in 1945, a considerable number of members, whose services had necessarily been retained during hostilities, took their discharge. The Force was left very much under establishment. To bring it up to strength, large scale recruiting was carried out during the years 1946 – 1947 from the traditional sources of the United Kingdom and South Africa.

The Royal visit of 1947 kept the BSAP fully occupied with security arrangements, general police and traffic duties. Southern Rhodesia was undergoing an unprecedented period of growth in population and expansion of industry and their Majesties' visit set the seal upon the tenor of the times.

By 1949, expansion of the Force was such that a policy of decentralization had to be introduced to relieve an over-burdened headquarters of routine matters. Accordingly, for police administrative purposes, the Colony was divided into three provinces: Mashonaland, Midlands and Matabeleland, each under the command of a senior officer. Later the provinces of Manicaland and Victoria were added.

The early 50s brought new problems by way of a general increase in crime and police duties. The efficiency of the Force kept in step with this expansion and, while it remained an armed force and military training still formed part of the syllabus for recruits, the accent, increasingly, was upon the essential functions of a civil force. Every endeavour was made to keep abreast of the times and with modern methods of crime-detection.

Early in 1953 a referendum was held in Southern Rhodesia to decide whether the Colony should join a proposed Federation of Rhodesia and Nyasaland. More than 85 per cent of the electorate went to the polls which resulted in a resounding *Yes* vote. On 1st August 1953, Federation was inaugurated through the appointment by proclamation of Lord Llewellin as the first Governor-General.

Prior to Federation the BSAP had been regarded as a military body and was trained both as mounted infantry and police. The aim had always been to change the image to that of an entirely civil police force. However, because of factors of manpower and limited finance, the Colony was not able to produce or maintain a standing army as such. With the Defence Act of 1926 an active Citizens Force (or Territorial Force) had been established, but this could not in any way be considered a standing army.

Thus the Police were still obliged to undertake the major role in defence of the Colony. Any adverse effects this dual role may have had on the Force's civil duties were overcome by a strict adherence to the practice of performing all constabulary duties unarmed. When Southern Rhodesia became associated with Northern Rhodesia and Nyasaland in a federal form of government, defence became the responsibility of the Federal Army and only then was the BSAP relieved of its duty as the first line of defence.

Jealous of its unique distinction from other colonial police forces, the BSAP remained the only law enforcement agency within Southern Rhodesia, responsible to the territorial Government but enforcing both Federal and Territorial Laws. As Salisbury was the capital of both the Colony of Southern Rhodesia and the Federation of

Rhodesia and Nyasaland, the Force performed certain functions on behalf of the Federal Government, such as escorts to His Excellency the Governor-General and ceremonial and security guard duties at his residence.

With Federation, it was hoped that the Force might be able to shed the last vestiges of militarism, but this hope was not to be fulfilled. Events in Africa and elsewhere brought home the realization that it was necessary to maintain a strong and efficient Police Force, trained in the use of arms. Indeed history has proved that in the context of Africa, a police force had of necessity to be a para-military organization.

In this period the issue of who should become the chieftain of the Banangwato tribe had reached such crisis proportions that Chief Seretse Khama was banished. During these difficult times the BSAP were called in on a number of occasions to assist the authorities in Bechuanaland. In 1953 a unit of the BSAP was sent to Nyasaland during disturbances occurring there. In the same year, several trained investigators were seconded to the Kenya Police when the activities of the *Mau Mau*[5] necessitated the declaration of an Emergency in that country.

In June 1953 a mounted contingent attended the coronation of Queen Elizabeth II, faithfully maintaining the reputation of the Corps. The Force was again occupied on a royal occasion in July of that year when, during the visit of Queen Elizabeth—the Queen Mother—and Princess Margaret, Her Majesty opened the Rhodes's Centenary Exhibition in Bulawayo.

The early years of Federation were relatively uneventful for the BSAP. It is true that for eight days there was a total strike of African labour at the Wankie Colliery in 1954 and a strike of European railway drivers and firemen later the same year, but firm government action in both cases soon brought matters to a close. The Police did their duty and good relations were maintained between the Force and the public, including strikers, throughout both emergencies. These good relations were to continue and become all the more commendable in the more difficult days at the end of Federation.

An event which stands out in this period was the signal honour conferred upon the Corps when in February 1954, Queen Elizabeth, the Queen Mother, consented to become the Honorary commissioner of the British South Africa Police, an office similar in every respect to that of Colonel-in-Chief of the Regiment.

---

5 An African terrorist organization.

BSA Police Crest 1949–1960

Plate 22. The British South Africa Police: First Sergeant 1953

The illustration portrays a sergeant wearing Dress Order No. I or full dress for the other ranks of the BSAP. This uniform representing the outcome of a number of changes made during the 1940s.

During the war procurement of suitable clothing and equipment was difficult. Generally a policy of *make-do* had to be applied. Such materials as were available were for the most part of the cheaper variety; khaki-drill, for example, being produced in a number of different shades. These unfortunate circumstances were reflected, more often than not, in ill-matched and ill-fitting uniforms. Despite urgent pleas to the overseas manufacturers, matters did not improve until 1948.

In 1943, initially as a wartime measure, bush tunics of the type issued to those members seconded for duty overseas, were supplied to the remainder of the European establishment. They nevertheless proved popular and by 1944 were on issue to African police as well. In March 1943 the blue tie replaced the khaki item which until then had been worn with khaki shirts. This, together with a blue cap-band, a blue lanyard and blue backing to rank badges, was a welcome innovation providing a distinctive touch to police uniforms at a time when the majority of Rhodesia's male population wore military dress in one form or another.

In 1944, good supplies having been obtained from England, a blue forage cap (*Cap Blue SD*) was accepted as another distinctive item of police uniform. In 1946, however, 100 caps of a new type of khaki-green gabardine were ordered—to be trialed as a possible replacement for both the blue service dress cap and the khaki field service cap. The trial item proved popular and, designated as the *Cap, Drab*, became a general issue to all European members in 1947. (It is worthy of note, however, that the blue cap was not dispensed with immediately, remaining on Ordnance Store shelves to make a brief re-appearance in 1957, when it was considered for wear with full dress. However, members' revulsion at the suggestion that they wear *Colonial Police* headgear saw to its prompt disposal elsewhere).

A green barathea jacket, with roll collar, recommended for wear in 1946, was finally introduced in 1948. With the new jacket came a new pattern leather waist-belt, with regimental clasp fashioned in the Boy Scout—*belt clasp, buckle sliding*—style. This belt was designed to be worn with or without a brace. When the brace was used, regulations prescribed that it was to be worn over the left shoulder to support, where necessary, a revolver carried in a leather holster on the right side. A small leather pouch designed to carry handcuffs and/or spare ammunition was intended for the left side of the belt, but like the revolver and holster it was rarely used, other than on ceremonial occasions, and hence fell into disuse. The remainder of the uniform remained unchanged.

Recruits under training who had not been issued with full dress paraded, on full-dress occasions, in a uniform comprising: Helmet (Universal), an open-neck khaki shirt, Jacket GS, Pantaloons BC, Leggings, Boots MS with spurs, and Belt with brace. The principal feature of this dress order, the Jacket GS had been introduced in 1948 and was made up in a khaki-green (drill) material with long sleeves and roll collar. On other than formal occasions, the Jacket GS was worn with Indian pattern shorts, i.e. shorts with a wide waistband having two buckles in support. (It has been suggested that there were die-hard conservatives in the Force who were of the opinion that the wearing of an open-necked shirt with *any* uniform too readily sacrificed smartness for comfort. A reason, perhaps, why this dress order also did not survive).

The Jacket GS was not long in use as a clothing item for European officers but, in a slightly different form, did remain in wear for African police until the introduction of terylene in the common uniform programme commenced in 1964.

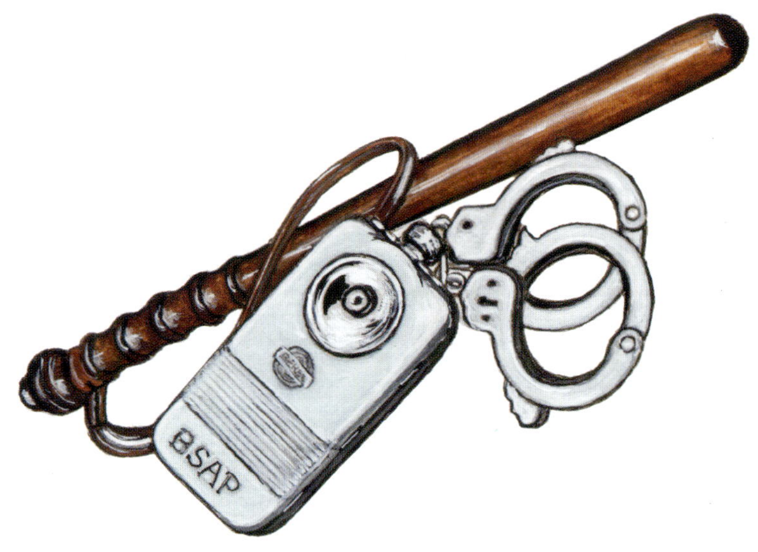

"Appointments" – BSAP (circa 1960)

Plate 22

The British South Africa Police: The African Policeman (Post 1950)

A considerable improvement in African education following the Second World War permitted the BSA Police to set higher standards of education, character and appearance for prospective African recruits. The resulting intakes of men (and later women) were consequently more receptive to training and courses of instruction became very much more comprehensive than was possible earlier.

By the early 1950s, the majority of those who applied to join the Force as constables possessed Standard VI qualifications and were proficient in reading and writing English. The Standard VI qualification and a height of 5 foot 8 inches became the minimum requirements for entry in 1958. The overall result was that Africans who had chosen the Force as a career began to play an ever-increasing role in policing the country.

Towards the end of 1947 a conference of African members of the Force considered the motion that the term *Native* was out-dated and in the circumstances undesirable. It was proposed that the Commissioner of Police be asked to change this designation. This was readily agreed to and by Force Order 919 of 1948 it was decreed that ranks previously having the prefix *Native* would thereafter be referred to as *African*. The nomenclature *African* was itself abandoned with the introduction of the Common Roll in 1965.

Over the years every endeavour was made to increase the spheres of activity and areas of responsibility allocated to the African policeman. Early in 1951 training began in the handling of four-wheeled vehicles and motor cycles. Typing was taught in the training school and at station level African members were encouraged to become more deeply involved in the investigation of crime. By 1952 the bulk of point duties for traffic control was in the hands of African Constables who acquitted themselves with considerable aplomb.

The rank of African Corporal was discontinued in 1953, those members holding this rank being reclassified as African Second Class Sergeants. Advancement was taken a stage further at the end of 1959 by the appointment of the first African Sub-Inspectors to the command of certain sub-stations. By a process of examination and selection from within the ranks of Sergeant-Major and Sub-Inspector a total of 91 African members of the Duty uniform Branch and the CID, including one woman, were promoted to the rank of Patrol Officer with effect from 1st September 1976. In the light of their increased responsibilities, 15 of this number were given Lance Section Officer rank in December of that year. The programme of advancement continued in 1978 when a number of the recently promoted Patrol Officers and Lance Section Officers achieved substantive promotion to Section Officer or the (by then) commissioned rank of Inspector. The rank of African Sub-Inspector fell away on 1st July 1978.

Matters of welfare were not ignored. Stress was placed on the improvement of housing, and the erection of family-type three-roomed cottages for the lower ranks proceeded as fast as finance and the availability of land would allow. The pole and daga hut encampment was soon to become very much a thing of the past.

The first school for the children of African policemen was started in the African Police Training School in 1937. This was to grow into a large modern educational establishment catering for children between the ages of six to 18 years. Teaching staff were attested members of the Force who worked under the supervision of the Ministry of Education. Eventually schools were provided in police camps in all the larger towns in Rhodesia, and in the smaller centres children attended either local government or mission schools or were boarded elsewhere.

Kuyedza clubs were inaugurated in August 1961 to provide social and educational courses for the wives of African members and ex-members of the Police and Police Reserve. In the Shona language *Kuyedza* means *to try* and the club so-named grew into a movement with branches throughout the country. Their endeavour was to educate in matters of hygiene and homecraft and to improve standards of living so as to permit African members and their families to take their place confidently in society.

The African Police Training School (APTS) later called Tomlinson Depot was provided with an Olympic-size swimming pool, a modern club, beer garden, tennis courts, a library and a general-dealers store, a spacious hall for cinema shows and other forms of entertainment. NCOs had their own mess, bar, reading and television rooms. Similar amenities were available at other accommodation camps in the police provinces and even the smallest station had its recreation club for African Police.

Plate 23. The British South Africa Police: African First Class Sergeant 1963

The Sergeant illustrated is wearing a uniform that made its first appearance when worn by African members performing duties directly concerned with the Royal Visit of 1947. It was in fact a version of the Jacket GS made over to accommodate the general physical dissimilarities between the African and European. This uniform was to become a general issue to African Police in 1948. Of khaki drill material and patterned closely on the bush shirt, it allowed for a collarless khaki shirt and long-sleeved jersey to be worn underneath if required. Always heavily starched, a high standard was required in the maintenance of the particular dress order and much time was spent in training with instruction in this regard. A common sight in the African Police Training School for many years was the so-called *Penguin Parade* of African recruits who, heading in line astern for the parade square, affected a peculiar stiff-legged waddle in order that their movement would not produce a crease in either their sleeves or trouser legs before the eagle eye of the Inspecting Officer passed over them.

The Helmet (Shako), similar in design to the German/Swiss helmet of 1900 – 1914 and that worn by the pre-war British postman, was first issued to African Police in 1941. Made of cork and covered in khaki drill material it served not only to protect the head from an unfriendly blow but from the effects of the sun as well. Phasing-out of the shako commenced with NCOs in 1964 and was completed in 1971.

Mounted service puttees had been issued to District Native Police since 1930, but were not worn by Town Police until 1941. This item was phased out at the commencement of the common uniform programme and replaced by brown leather leggings and stockings (Blue Topped).

Boots (Brown Leather, AP) had been on issue to District Mounted Native Police since the end of the First World War, but were not part of the scale of issue to other African members until received by Town Native Police in November 1941. District Native Police at that time were issued with sandals of the type issued to other ranks of the Indian Army. These were cool and functional but, mainly as a result of a question of prestige, were not a popular item of wear. District Native Police were issued with boots at the end of World War II. (It is of interest to note that over the past half-century, as the wearing of boots and shoes by African children became a more common practice, the sizes in footwear issued to African police have generally reduced until today they approximate those of the European).

The figure in the accompanying illustration is portrayed as wearing the crown and chevrons appropriate to a member who was above the efficiency barrier in the rank of sergeant and who, prior to the introduction of the Common Roll, was known as a First Sergeant. Badges of rank and buttons were made of brass until the beginning of 1961 when they were replaced by those of a gold anodized material. The introduction of anodized button, badges and insignia proved a great boon to members of the Force, as it greatly reduced the time and labour spent in producing a smart turnout. Black plastic backing material for belt numerals and other insignia was a temporary affectation of the early 1960s.

As a result of the Packard Report the issue of a common uniform to both European and African policemen began in 1964 with the distribution of barathea forage caps to African NCOs, and trench-coats to all ranks as stocks of waterproof coats and greatcoats were exhausted. The chain attached to whistle was phased out in 1969 and replaced by the blue lanyard as worn by European members. The next stage was the issue of whipcord uniforms for winter wear, followed by terylene uniforms to replace those made of khaki drill. The whole exercise was completed in 1971.

Badge, Helmet, African Police 1961

Plate 23

THE YEARS BETWEEN 1959 and 1964 were among the most difficult ever endured by the BSAP, regrettably foreshadowing greater stresses in the years to come. Urged on by the *Winds of Change*, the flood-tide of African nationalism sweeping down from the north, boiled over into Northern Rhodesia and Nyasaland and flowed remorselessly into Southern Rhodesia. In the wake of a campaign of civil disobedience the first of a series of *Emergencies* was declared in 1959. Notwithstanding its own heavy commitments, the Force responded to a further request from the Nyasaland Government and sent a contingent to that country to assist in the maintenance of law and order.

The years that followed saw the rise and fall of African nationalist political parties, competing with one another in acts of violence and intimidation, until their activities reached such proportion that the Government found it necessary to impose a ban upon them. Intimidation, assaults, damage to property, petrol bomb attacks, even murder, were acts perpetrated against the civil populace, in particular the African, with the object of inflaming opinion against a properly constituted Government.

The Force, as was to be expected, responded magnificently to the strains placed upon it. The security situation demanded very long hours of work from most members. Though home-life and recreation were disrupted, these and other difficulties were borne with cheerful determination. Some African members of the Force were subjected to intimidation, but to their great credit stood firm. The majority of the African population had no wish to contravene the law, but were subjected to pressure when they co-operated with the authorities. Individually they retained their natural ebullience and continued to respect the police and to approach the Force for assistance and protection in adversity. En masse and under the influence of inflammatory speeches at times a mob hysteria took over and naturally good relations suffered.

Unfortunately, during riots in this period, the BSAP lost its proud record of over 50 years, of not using firearms or of killing anyone in any outbreak of civil disorder. In the circumstances it was inevitable. Firm and immediate action was necessary to avoid the spread of hooliganism that, if unchecked in its early stages, could have led to a complete breakdown of law and order. The few casualties that were inflicted are indicative of the strict control exercised by the police when conditions made the use of firearms imperative.

Eventually and for a space of time, the tide turned. Police activity was followed by a marked lessening of tension. The introduction of more stringent legislation in the form of the Law and Order Maintenance Act and the rustication of political extremists led to a sharp decrease in politically inspired crime.

Apart from matters of politics, the following domestic events of note occurred during this period: In 1959 CID Headquarters moved from Bulawayo to Salisbury to occupy quarters vacated by Police General Headquarters which had returned to its wartime home in Milton House. On 30th May 1960, history was made when the Honorary Commissioner, Her Majesty Queen Elizabeth the Queen Mother, reviewed 2,300 men and women of the Force in the grounds of the Police Depot in Salisbury. Later the same year the City of Salisbury honoured the Force by conferring upon it the Freedom of Entry into the city, at a ceremony held in the gardens of the Town House. This latter ceremony which occurred on 12th September 1960 was performed exactly 70 years from the date upon which the BSA Company's Police and the Pioneer Column had arrived at the site of the future capital city.

In 1961, because of the considerable increase in the duties and responsibilities involved in policing the capital, the City of Salisbury and its surrounding area was taken out of the Police province of Mashonaland and created a province in its own right.

In 1962 a survey of the force was conducted by Lieutenant-General Sir Charles Douglas Packard with broad terms of reference. This led to the change in structure that occurred in September 1963. Among other things, Southern Rhodesia was divided into six police provinces and areas previously designated as sub-districts were promoted to full District status with their own officers in command.

On 31st December 1963 the Federation of Rhodesia and Nyasaland formally dissolved —a magnificent concept capitulating to political intransigence.

Plate 24. The British South Africa Police: Patrol Officer (Riot Duty) 1965

Although training in the use of small arms had always been one of the disciplines of the BSAP, exercises in the use of riot weapons and crowd control did not figure largely in police training syllabi until 1930, when experiments with tear gas were carried out in the Depot.

As it was primarily a mounted force, it was natural that any training in and methods of crowd control should be based mainly upon the horse and the principal riot weapon of the day, the Lathi. The Lathi, of Anglo-Indian origin, was a slim bamboo cane approximately four feet long, weighted and bound with leather at one end and having a leather hand-guard and carry-thong at the other. When mounted, this weapon was carried on saddle-furniture in a position normally occupied by the sword. Recruits in the Depot practised mounted riot drill with Lathis as recently as the late 1950s. For protection against missiles the helmet universal was worn and, when dismounted, a wickerwork shield was carried.

In 1954 a permanent riot stand-by party was formed from Depot personnel. This was later augmented and ultimately replaced by parties made up of men drawn from all urban and suburban stations in the Salisbury area on a weekly roster basis. The same system was followed at all major centres throughout the Colony. Stand-by parties were equipped with steel helmets, riot shields, batons, tear gas and other riot weapons. Normal dress orders of the day were worn, with the addition of haversacks and water bottles. Personal weapons were available but held in reserve.

In March 1954 *Emergency and Musketry Dress*, commonly called *Riot Kit* was first issued. As the illustration shows, this was of blue *drill* material, patterned upon British Army Battle Dress, and worn with blue web belt and gaiters of military pattern. Military pattern (green) web pouches were added to carry gas grenades and, on the chest, a respirator. Anti-gas goggles, when used, were carried slung around the neck of the wearer. The steel helmet was replaced by a fibreglass helmet of similar pattern in January 1960 and this, in turn, was replaced later the same year by the fibreglass helmet of the type illustrated. A grey shirt was worn under the riot jacket in winter and in place of it in warmer weather. Latterly, Boots Combat (Mars) were worn in preference to Boots MS or AP and the web gaiters. More often than not, however, riot stand-by parties were instructed to wear the dress order of the day in order to emphasize the *police* (i.e. *minimum force*) nature of its role.

The Patrol Officer is shown as carrying a grenade launcher based upon a No.1 (Mark 3) SMLE rifle that is bound with copper wire for strengthening and support. Later cup-dischargers were made available for the FN rifle and specialized riot guns and crowd control equipment together with a variety of gas projectiles, grenades, etc., formed part of the anti-riot and crowd control arsenal.

With the introduction of the Common Roll in 1965, Inspectors and Chief Inspectors of the Force resumed as badges of rank the military stars or *pips* that had been taken from them in 1948. In the intervening period they had worn on each shoulder strap, bars denoting rank which were of a style similar to that affected by junior officers in the armed forces of the United States of America. European Constables, who until that time had worn no distinguishing badge of rank, became Patrol Officers and wore either one or two bars depending upon whether they were above or below the efficiency barrier in that rank. European First and Second Class Sergeants assumed the rank of Section Officers, wearing three bars on each epaulette to denote their rank.

Member – Riot Standby Party 1960

Plate 24

The Depot

The BSA Police Depot was established in the Rhodesian capital, Salisbury in 1896 when Police moved from their original camp in what was later to become Cecil Square.

Standing to the northeast of the city centre, hard by Government House and the leafy Avenues, the Police Camp (its usual title) covered an area of some 130 hectares. Entering the precincts of Morris Depot by either the North or Montague Avenue gates, even ordinary mortals could not help but be impressed by its unique atmosphere—notwithstanding the hustle and bustle of a cantonment at times engaged in the prosecution of war or other lesser emergencies. Pleasantly laid out in a manner reminiscent of an old-style cavalry depot, with its well-kept open spaces, trim hedges and majestic trees,[4] the Depot represented the home and very centre of the traditions of the Force. Named after Brigadier John Sydney Morris, CBE, Commissioner of Police and wartime Inspector-General of Defence Forces, it was an establishment that provided modern barracks and utilities that contrasted with and yet complemented fine old regimental buildings redolent of history.

4 The contrast with the establishment presently located (circ.1999) would to an old-timer be heart-breaking.

Flagstaff & Plinth (Montagu Ave entrance BSA Police Depot, Salisbury)

On the extremities could be found the service departments: the Pioneers, Provost, Marine Workshops, etc., and to the south the *Hampton Stables*[5], Farriers, grooming and sick-lines for horses and mules. Fronting the Regimental Institute and Mess was the so-called *Green Square*, often the scene of colourful ceremonial and recruit pass-out parades. At the northern end of the green square, flanked by two flagstaffs, stood the *Blatherwick Memorial*, an obelisk dedicated to the memory of James Blatherwick, the Corps' first Regimental Sergeant Major. At regular intervals throughout the day, trumpeters would take post at the memorial to sound calls, familiar to cavalrymen, which marked the passage of time. Behind the memorial and an avenue lined with palm trees, was the Officers' Mess, first located on that site in 1897 and a veritable treasure-house of Force history.

To the east lay Tomlinson Depot, the African Police Training School, likewise named after a former Commissioner of Police, Lieutenant-Colonel A.J. Tomlinson. Here where emphasis was placed upon the moulding of character and on fostering a sense of responsibility, in six short months, raw young African recruits were turned into the qualified and highly respected *Mapolisa*.

To the Rhodesian public, perhaps the best known part of the Depot, was the Police Club and its beautiful sports ground, the venue for major international sporting events. In days past, while thousands might make the trek to witness the *Springboks* or *All Blacks* at play, rarely were larger crowds seen than on those crisp August days when the BSAP put on its *Annual Mounted Sports and Display*. Basically a military tattoo, but with peculiarly (Rhodesian) police embellishments, the Display represented an *open day* for the Depot and for the police service as a whole. A regular feature until 1973, when operational commitments forced it into abeyance, the Display dated back to a pageant performed in May 1943 which was a feature of a *Happy Hampstead* fête put on

5 Named for a well respected *Riding Master* (See Plate 17).

The Regimental Institute – BSA Police Depot, Salisbury

in support of war-time charities. To many the highlight of the Display was the musical ride performed by the senior squad of recruits under training in the Morris Depot, that included such movements as *The St George's Cross*, *The Wheel* and counter-trot, usually climaxing with a spectacular *Figure of Eight* that delighted the crowd.

As the Senior Service in Rhodesia, it was the proud and unique privilege of the Force to provide ceremonial escorts for State occasions—such as, for example, the *Opening of Parliament*. One of the first ceremonial escorts performed by the BSAP was undertaken on the occasion of the visit to Salisbury of their Royal Highnesses, the Prince and Princess of Conaught, on 16th August 1921. Other royal escorts were occasioned by the visit of HRH The Prince of Wales in 1925 and later by the royal visits of 1947, 1953 and 1960. During the Second World War the First Reserve of the BSAP provided a mounted escort for Sir Evelyn Baring KCMG, on his first visit to Bulawayo as Governor. The first Presidential Escort was performed on 28th May 1970 for the opening of the first parliamentary session of the Republic of Rhodesia.

In so-called progressive times, there were those who considered that the presence of horses in a Police Training Depot an anachronism. Such critics were very soon reminded, however, that a horseman requires qualities of self-discipline, stamina and teamwork, surely quintessential qualities for a policeman. That the horse still had a useful role to play was proved by the resurrection of the Mounted Unit for deployment on active counter-insurgency duties.

And would not much of the splendour of State Occasions have been lost had the BSA Police Mounted Escort been excluded?

The Blatherwick Memorial – BSA Police Depot, Salisbury

THE DAWN OF January 1st, 1964, ushered in not only a new year but a new era in the history of Rhodesia and, necessarily, that of the BSAP. The Federation of the Rhodesias and Nyasaland had died at midnight and with its demise the two northern territories had automatically achieved independence. Southern Rhodesia, whose right to the same status was irrefutable, remained a colony. As a result, Rhodesia suddenly found itself thrust upon the world stage as a succession of protracted but unproductive discussions took place between the Colonial Office and Rhodesian delegations. Whilst as individuals the men and women of the BSAP were vitally concerned with the outcome of such negotiations, which would have a material effect upon their lives and future careers, the Force itself remained concerned only with upholding the law without political or racial bias.

A marked decrease in politically inspired offences had brought the crime situation back to normal, but the BSAP, in common with police forces throughout the world, was severely handicapped by a shortage of manpower. The need to provide 24-hour coverage for seven days a week, particularly in the major centres, had the result of reducing the effective strength of the Force to a quarter of its establishment. The consequent inadequate beat coverage was partially compensated in 1964 by the formation of Crime Prevention Units employed on plain-clothes patrols and observation duties in liaison with the CID and other police units.

A new Police Act and Regulations came into effect in February 1965. These not only consolidated and brought up to date existing legislation, but introduced a number of new features among which, for example, the rank structure of the Force was changed to permit two points of entry, depending upon educational and other qualifications, to a common promotion roll for both European and African members.

Whilst, as impartial upholders of the law, a police service must—and in the case of the British South Africa Police certainly did—remain aloof from politics, political events that shape the history and development of a country cannot but have an effect upon the force that serves it. In Rhodesia, where it was said with some pride that the history of the BSAP was that of Rhodesia, and vice versa, this was indeed the case.

Negotiations between the Rhodesian and British Government finally were aborted and the Rhodesian Prime Minister, Ian Smith, took the bold—some might say foolhardy—step of unilaterally declaring Rhodesia's independence on 11th November 1965. In a final act of governance, the invidiously circumstanced Governor, Sir Humphrey Gibbs, enjoined members of the Force to remain at their posts and to maintain order and public safety.

Plate 25. The British South Africa Police: Patrol Officer (Mounted Escort) 1968

The first functional unit of Mounted Police was the London Bow Street Horse Patrol established in 1758. From that time, police in England began to take over the control of civil disorder from the army. Chartist rioting in the late 1830s initiated the formation of standing units of Mounted Police and their employment in the keeping of public order, to regulate processions, ceremonial and other large gatherings, as well as normal street patrols.

The concept of the mounted policeman which coalesced sympathetically with the concept of minimum force (as well, it must be admitted, with the idea of limiting costs) was readily taken up throughout the British Empire and elsewhere in the western world. In North America, northern India and southern Africa, problems of lawlessness and disorder were mainly concerned with the activities of freebooters and cross-border raiders and their impact upon indigenous peoples. In Rhodesia, as in Canada but a short time earlier, it was the mounted policeman who brought law and order to a vast interland.

It is not surprising, therefore, that the dress and equipment of the latter-day Mounted Policeman has its roots in both cavalry and Force traditions.

The Patrol Officer illustrated is shown wearing the military-style Full Dress, consisting of a barathea tunic—a post-war adaptation of the pre-war Greens—and bedford-cord riding breeches (Pantaloons BC) adapted from a style introduced in the 1920s. In addition, he is wearing a white universal helmet (i.e. bleached white and blancoed) and highly polished escort gauntlets. Carrying a lance with its blue and gold pennant flying and mounted upon an immaculately groomed troop horse, a member of a mounted escort troop, in full panoply, was truly a fine sight to behold.

The lance dates back to the earliest of times as a weapon for horsemen. It was abolished as a weapon of war by British Army Order 392 of 1927, but retained by Lancer Regiments of the British and British-Indian armies for ceremonial purposes.

Bridle Boss

Regimental Orders of 1900 indicate that provision was made for the BSAP to carry the lance when escorting the Administrator of the Colony. However, the writer has been unable to find any evidence to confirm that this ever occurred. Nevertheless, had a lance been carried at that time, it would have been with red over white pennon—as was the case with the Rhodesia Horse in 1897. *The Outpost*[6] of January 1943 has photographs of the BSAP Mounted Escort that greeted the arrival of the Governor-Designate, Sir Evelyn Baring on 10th December 1942, and records:

> *Of particular interest to the Force was the Mounted Escort's use of lances instead of rifles. There can be no doubt of the change being in every way a vast improvement, not only from the point of view of appearance, but also from the strain imposed upon the Escort over long distances and long periods of waiting.*

The lances employed by the BSAP were of male bamboo, eight feet in length with chromed steel point and butt and bearing a blue over gold pennon, crimped after the fashion of the 16th Lancers. In the illustration, the lance rests in a bucket attached to the off-stirrup and is held at the carry.

Saddle furniture carried by an escort troop horse comprised a universal saddle, with saddle wallets, breastplate connecting straps and breastplate, over a ceremonial saddlecloth or shabrack. The shabrack was made up of either blue serge or blue melton cloth, with gold oak-leaf facings and bearing the regimental badge in gold and silver wire embroidery. It was lined with saddler's-check serge cloth with white canvas duck stiffening. The breastplate consisted of a gold-plated helmet badge upon a leather shield. The bridle-boss was a circular brass boss bearing the regimental device surrounded by the inscription: *BSA Police*. Stirrup leathers had ornamental chrome runners that also bore the regimental crest. A white headrope completed the equipment.

---

6 Regimental Magazine of the British South Africa Police.

Saddle Furniture Ceremonial

Troop Horses of the BSAP were for the most part half to three quarter bred from the Kimberley or Mooi River Districts of South Africa, together with a fair sprinkling of the better Karroo type[7]. They were brought in at three to four years of age, usually unbroken. Prospective Troop Horses underwent intensive training by the Police Remount Section for a period of nine to ten months where particular attention was given to temperament. Those showing any signs of instability were quickly weeded out. The average working life of a police horse was 12 to 14 years whereafter they were secured to quiet retirement.

BSAP Troop Horses had hogged manes and tails that fell to a uniform (half-hock) length.

---

7 Similar to the Australian "Brumby".

Superintendent Dress Order No. 2 1972

Plate 25

THE ASSUMPTION OF independence and subsequent declaration of a State of Emergency involved the police in many additional duties. Fortunately, in what might have been a difficult period, all remained generally peaceful and the crime rate normal. 1965 was a year full of political tension and uncertainty but the Force was unswerving in the performance of its duties. As a result the high degree of public support and confidence enjoyed by the Corps among people of all races and persuasions was sustained and even enhanced in some sectors.

In 1966 a number of well-armed and equipped gangs of terrorists entered Rhodesia from territories to the north, with the avowed intention of subverting government and creating chaos. Such armed aggression continued spasmodically through the years 1967 and 1968. On each occasion, the threat was met with singular success by the combined Rhodesian Security Forces that achieved the almost total elimination of the attackers before they were able to carry out their various missions.

It is often a convenient euphemism to refer to terrorists as *Freedom Fighters* or some other such virtuous or high sounding title but, to the Police of the time, those who made war upon unarmed civilians and committed unprovoked attacks upon private and public property, were criminals to be dealt with according to law. Those who surrendered were arrested; others who resisted were not so fortunate. The capture of terrorists placed an additional burden upon the members of the Force responsible for criminal investigations, for each was dealt with by normal process, entailing investigation as well as interrogation of a specialized nature requiring skills of a high professional standard, often continuing for weeks after the particular operation in the field had ended.

To combat terrorist activity, training and counter-insurgency methods were adjusted to permit rapid deployment both to and within affected areas. Police Anti-Terrorist Units (PATU) were evolved from the earlier Tracker Combat Teams and VATs (Volunteers for Advanced Training), with the special objective of hunting down terrorists, arresting or eliminating them.

The Declaration of Independence startled the world and was viewed with marked displeasure by the British Government. Overnight police and populace alike had become rebels and sanctions were implemented against them. In order to maintain standards and efficiency the Force was obliged to join the ranks of sanction-busters and to encourage local manufacturers to meet its various needs. Despite talks, talks about talks, negotiations on the warships *Tiger* and *Fearless* and the application of both physical and psychological pressures, the Rhodesian and British Governments remained estranged.

A result not expected by the enemies of Rhodesia in their attacks upon the economy and integrity of the country, was that from a population of widely divergent racial and political identities, a colony very soon became a nation united in the will to survive. The symbol of that nationhood, Rhodesia's own green and white flag, was raised for the first time at ceremonies held simultaneously throughout the country at 9.00 am on Independence Day, Monday 11th November 1968. At the same time the flag was raised to the masthead at all police headquarters, stations and posts as well as military, air force and other government establishments throughout the country.

The Rhodesia General Service Medal was introduced in November 1969, as an award to members of the security forces serving during terrorist incursions since April 1966. The issue of this medal presaged the issue of wholly Rhodesian honours and awards in November 1970 that included a Police Cross for Conspicuous Gallantry, the Police Decoration for Gallantry, a Police Cross for Distinguished Service and new medals for meritorious and long service to replace the former colonial police medals[6].

Rhodesia became a Republic at midnight on 2nd March 1970, an event that was ushered in as quietly and with as little melodrama as the Declaration of Independence five years earlier.

6 The police medals and awards were designed (or in some cases re-designed) by the author.

Plate 26. The British South Africa Police: Patrol Officer (Dog Handler) 1969

The Dog Handler is depicted wearing BSA Police Dress Order No. 3—worn by members of the Force when they performed ordinary police duties in towns, attended magistrates' court, parades or other duties (as ordered). It comprised a cap (SD Drab), a short-sleeved khaki terylene suit—worn with blue lanyard securing a whistle—and belt, leggings and boots of brown leather.

The terylene uniform, first issued in 1960, dispensed with the daily washing and starching required by the old-pattern khaki drill. Terylene did not shrink, it was hard wearing and easy to wash and iron. Although it did not present with the sharpness of newly starched drill, it was cooler to wear and stayed fresh looking and smart for a longer period.

The brace fitting for the belt, formerly issued for wear by Section Officers, Patrol Officers and Station Sergeants, was withdrawn from use in August 1966. It served no useful purpose and often proved to be a hazard when effecting a difficult arrest. It was retained, however, for ceremonial motor cycle and mounted escort duties.

With Rhodesia's Unilateral Declaration of Independence, came the imposition of sanctions. For a time all sorts of difficulties were encountered in the supply of uniforms and equipment. Traditionally, much of this had come from the United Kingdom, now the principal antagonist. Such difficulties were overcome by a vigorous campaign to encourage local production that was very successful. So successful, in fact, that the local product proved superior to the equivalent imported item. As of January 1966 it could be said that adequate supplies of clothing materials and necessary metalwork, such as buttons, badges, etc., were to hand. In addition, as well as the manufacture of leggings and undertaking all boot and shoe repairs for the Force, the Police Saddlers fabricated and supplied all items of saddlery and leather-work required for both the men and animals on strength.

Dogs were first used by the BSAP after the First World War, but only for a short period. Their success was limited and the belief arose that environmental conditions in Rhodesia were insurmountable. Their employment, therefore, was discontinued. However, as the result of successes achieved by a member of the CID using his own dog to track down criminals, the idea was revised and by 1945 dogs were again considered for police work. A Tracker Dog Section of the CID was formed and, by the mid-1950s, the results achieved in the detection and apprehension of criminals were such as to justify the extension of their services to all police provinces.

The Police Dog Handlers Section was formed in 1958, providing trained dogs with European handlers of the Duty Uniformed Branch for beat-work in the larger centres. African dog handlers commenced training in 1961 and in 1962 the section was reorganized, divorced from the CID, and placed under the command of an officer of the Duty Branch. Thereafter, dogs were used extensively throughout the country, not only for tracking purposes, but for crowd control and the maintenance of law and order generally where their utility and efficiency were unparalleled.

Guard Dogs for border stations were introduced in 1965 and with the onset of terrorist incursions the section provided dogs and handlers for anti-terrorist operations. Dogs continued to be used successfully in the operational areas until the end of the guerrilla war, both for following up spoor and locating terrorist equipment. In counter-insurgency operations a dog handler would wear combat clothing, and while training, either grey shirt and shorts or white combination overalls.

Plate 26

THE YEARS 1969, 1970 AND 1971 were comparatively uneventful and a period marked by a lull in the incidence of terrorist incursions and contacts with armed gangs. These halcyon days were not to continue, for in January 1972 the presence of the Pearce Commission[7] precipitated an eruption of politically motivated violence which was subdued by police, but not before considerable damage had been done to property in the African townships. With the departure of the Commission the situation returned to normal.

Unhappily, events during December 1972 led to the discovery that insurgents had become well entrenched in the remote rural areas of Rhodesia's north-eastern borders. Land mines and anti-personnel bombs were set to kill and maim road users, and sneak attacks were made upon isolated homesteads. In 1973, their entry to Rhodesia facilitated by the generally uncontrollable state of affairs in Mozambique, terrorists turned their attention to tribal areas and commenced a campaign of brutality and terror aimed at coercing the unwilling African inhabitants. In this they achieved a great deal of success, for even the most sophisticated of the indigenous population were inherently susceptible to intimidation.

The National Service Act of 1976 permitted the BSAP to select from among the best of Rhodesian youth for service with the Force. Barred from recruiting in the United Kingdom, the Force was grateful for this input of local material. Many of those inducted were extremely young, but considering the comparatively short time available to train and to mould them as individuals able to cope with the demands that would be made upon them, the results were more than gratifying. The first in-takes of National Service Patrol Officers entering the Depot in July were posted to stations in the following October, where they were to provide a much-needed boost to available manpower. With urban terrorism a constant threat, the Special Constabulary scheme was re-vitalized with an encouraging response, in their turn, from men in the older age groups with no prior military or police commitment.

The granting of independence to Mozambique on 25th July 1975 further exacerbated the Rhodesian security situation. A malevolently hostile border necessitated operational counter-measures in the eastern part of the country. At this time the BSAP were happy to receive assistance from units of the South African Police whose government was intent upon maintaining a buffer between its own borders and those of the hostile states to the north.

The major event of 1976 was Prime Minister Ian Smith's meeting with American Secretary of State Kissinger, on 19th September. This led to the acceptance of the infamous *Package Deal*—which the Geneva Conference later that year disclosed to be no deal at all.

A full cycle in police activity occurred toward the end of 1976 with the formation and training of a Police Mounted Unit—distinct from and in addition to the Ceremonial

7 Lord Pearce: Commission to determine the acceptability of the terms of the Smith/Home agreement.

Escort Troop and the Remount Unit. Destined to fulfil tasks similar to those of the patrolling troopers of bygone years, by establishing a police presence in the less accessible areas of the country, the Unit succeeded in playing a valuable part in counter-insurgency operations. The year, 1976, also saw the introduction of a Police Reserve Marine Division to meet a requirement for increased patrolling on Lake Kariba.

Terrorist incursions escalated in the years 1977 and 1978. Despite its economic and sociological problems, Rhodesia's war against the communist ideologue was being prosecuted with vigour and, in terms of contact between opposing forces, was being won. However, in the 20th century, wars are fought with machinery. The *engines of war* demand logistical support and, more than anything else, require fuel. It was, therefore, a somewhat unhappy irony that it should be Rhodesia's principal supporter who, in the final analysis, was to bring this particular war to an end by denying its ally access to petroleum and oil.

Plate 27. The British South Africa Police: Assistant Commissioner 1970

In the light of the planned Federation between Southern Rhodesia, Northern Rhodesia and Nyasaland, police committees deliberated assiduously upon the prospect of de-militarization, the possibility of amalgamation with other police forces into a federal organization and consequent changes in the dress and to the rank structure of the Force. As it happened, Federation, which left the BSAP intact, had little effect. The on-going civil role of police, however, was underlined by a de-militarization of police rank titles.

The BSA Company's Police, as semi-military formations, had military ranks. Concession was made to their police role by the titles: Chief Inspector, Inspector, etc., for junior officers; nevertheless, their ranks were still afforded a local military equivalent. The object and intent was maintained through the amalgamations of 1903 and 1909 when the officer cadre wore the following military badges: Chief Inspector (Crown); Inspector (3 Stars); Sub-Inspector (2 Stars) and Acting Sub-Inspector (1 Star).

With the onset of the Great War, military titles were again paramount and in 1920 the ranks of the Inspectorate were relegated to Warrant Officer status, while those of Commissioned Officer ranged upward from Acting Lieutenant to Colonel. During the Second World War a decision was made to drop military titles for official purposes although certain officers retained them in their private lives to the consequent confusion of the public. Shortly after the war military ranks were restored.

Government Notice No 304 of 1954 introduced new police ranks of Commissioner, Deputy Commissioner, Senior Assistant Commissioner, Assistant Commissioner, Chief Superintendent and Superintendent. Officers were again permitted to retain their former military titles but, by common consent, had dropped them entirely by 1958.

The Senior Officer illustrated is shown wearing *Patrols*—a form of full-dress uniform introduced in 1948 to serve all commissioned ranks in place of the mess kit which had fallen into disuse with the advent of war.

Patrols were intended for wear on ceremonial and other full-dress occasions. The Dress Order comprised a Patrol Jacket of blue serge material and overalls of blue barathea with a stripe of gold melton cloth, one and three quarter inches wide, running down the outer seams. The cap was also of blue-black barathea, having a black patent-leather peak and cap band of black oak-leaf pattern melton cloth. Officers of or above the rank of Senior Assistant Commissioner wore a single line of gold-oak-leaf embroidery upon the cap-peak and the Commissioner of Police two lines of embroidery[8]. The Cap badge

8 From September 1953, Assistant and Senior Assistant Commissioners wore the single line of gold oak-leaf embroidery and the Deputy Commissioners and Commissioner the double line.

was of gold and silver wire upon a background of dark blue cloth. The belt of gold oak-leaf pattern lace upon a soft, blue coloured, leather base two and one-quarter inches deep, supported a gilded ceremonial sword. The belt-buckle consisted of a gilt rectangular plate with burnished edges three and a quarter inches wide by two and a half inches deep, bearing the regimental badge surmounted by a crown. The lanyard was of gold wire. Gorget patches, appropriate to rank, were silver wire embroidery upon a light blue base. Badges of rank were of white metal. Boots, black half-Wellington, with box spurs and white doeskin gloves completed the ensemble.

The original police officer's mess kit consisted of a blue serge jacket with roll collar, gold-cloth epaulettes, gilt badges and buttons, worn with a white shirt, white linen collar and black silk tie together with overalls of blue serge having one and a half inch black oak-leaf braid on the outer seams. As stated earlier, mess kit fell into disuse but was re-introduced in the early 1960s. In its final form, *Mess Kit* consisted of a mess jacket of plain black venetian cloth with shoulder straps of self material; a buff coloured waistcoat; blue-black barathea overalls (trousers with plain bottoms narrowed at the knees and flaring slightly to cover the boot) with one and a half inch gold melton oak-leaf braid down the side seams; gilt metal collar badges and gold anodized badges of rank. On less formal occasions, the white dress shirt and waistcoat were dispensed with in favour of a soft-collared shirt and cummerbund of regimental pattern. Boots, black, half-Wellington had box inserts in the centre heel to accept swan-necked spurs.[9]

The Packard Survey of 1962 determined that the wearing of Patrols tended to accentuate the gap between officers and other ranks and that, as officers had mess kit, there was no purpose in retaining it. As a compromise, however, the wearing of Patrols was restricted to officers of and above the rank of Assistant Commissioner with effect from September 1963. From that date, on appropriate occasions, Senior Assistant Commissioners and above wore the following:

Patrols with ceremonial sword, scabbard and belt gold wire, gold wire lanyard, blue cap with gold melton band, white doeskin gloves, half-Wellington boots, spurs and court-mounted medals.

Assistant Commissioners wore the same with the following exceptions:

Nickel-plated sword hilt and scabbard, gold cotton cloth belt and lanyard and white cotton gloves.

Chief Superintendents and below, on the relevant occasions, would wear Dress Order No. 2.

The use of silver wire embroidery and white metal buttons and badges on patrols was discontinued in October 1969 when such items were replaced with gilt wire

---

9 Swan necked spurs are made of solid brass with a steel tongue. The spur is 100mm long by 80mm at its widest part. On each side of the open ends of the spur are false screw heads. The rowel of the spur is made of round, ribbed brass which is designed to spin.

embroidery and gold anodized buttons. By 1971, as a result of UDI[10] insignia bearing the royal crown had been replaced with new items displaying the traditional Rhodesian lion and tusk emblem or, in some cases, the Zimbabwe bird.

10 Rhodesia's Unilateral Declaration of Independence

Superintendent (Mess Kit) 1980

Plate 27

Cadets and Women Police

A caption in the March 1934 edition of *The Outpost* announced: *Cadets are with us.*

Government Notice No. 34 of 1934 had created a Cadet Branch for the British South Africa Police providing the opportunity of a head start for Rhodesian youth considering a career in their country's police service. Traditionally, Rhodesians, like others of the colonial breed, while ever ready for a "stoush" or to volunteer when there was a job to be done in war or other emergency, were not prone to list for service in the *regular* forces of either the military or police. Southern Rhodesia generally, and the BSAP in particular, relied upon recruitment from the United Kingdom. Unfortunately, this Cadet project too was to founder on the rock of disinclination. After some initial enthusiasm interest waned and the scheme had to be abandoned temporarily in 1936. Nevertheless, members of the early Cadet branch continued to serve, some obtaining senior rank in the Corps in later years.

In 1956 the Cadet scheme was revived. Once again the intention was to encourage young people to join the Force when they left school at 16 or 17 years of age. With commendable foresight it was considered that traditional recruiting grounds might not always be open. Young Rhodesians were keen enough, and of the right material, but until the re-introduction of Cadets, were often lost to the Force through having to start work immediately they left school. More often than not, this meant that by the time they had reached the age of 18, and were old enough to join the Police, they had settled upon different career paths that they were then loath to leave.

During June 1956 an extensive recruiting tour of the Colony promoting the Force as a career made particular reference to the newly created Cadet Branch. The immediate results were applications to join from over 100 boys. It was from these that the nucleus of the Branch was formed. From that time on, there was a steady stream of school-leavers attesting as cadets, the majority continuing to serve as regulars upon attaining the minimum age. In January 1962 an African Police Cadet scheme was initiated. Originally it catered for the sons of serving members of the Force only, but later the scheme was enlarged to include all African boys with the required qualifications. Both cadet schemes, over the years, proved very successful and were to verify the dictum—*Catch 'em whilst they're young.*

Before the Second World War there was generally a belief that police duties were far too strenuous ever to be undertaken by members of the so called *weaker sex*. This notion changed, however, when the war left the Colony with but a handful of police to maintain law and order. Naturally, it was difficult to obtain male recruits; but the solution was to hand with the advent of Women's Auxiliary Services. Notwithstanding the concept was initially applied to military forces only, in July 1941 it was decided to establish the Southern Rhodesia Women's Auxiliary Police Service (SRWAPS). There was no difficulty in finding recruits, for women were ready and eager to play their part in the war effort.

Early misgivings concerning the suitability of women in a police role were soon dispelled and in a remarkably short space of time those appointed attained a standard of efficiency that compared very favourably with that of their male counterparts. That the advent of policewomen was popular in the Force was epitomized by the trooper who from his lonely district police station wrote to the Editor of *The Outpost*: *... the introduction of WAPS will bring us something we have needed for years*! One can but hope that his prayers were answered.

In the beginning, a woman Superintendent was in charge of the SRWAPS and weekly drill parades were a regular feature. The appearance of these trim and attractive young women "on parade" unfailingly drew applause from appreciative onlookers. The war over, however, and in common with other wartime auxiliary units, the SRWAPS was disbanded in 1945. All efforts were then concentrated upon building the regular force up to full strength—but the outstanding service rendered by the women's service during the war was not forgotten.

In 1947 it was considered that women could rightly expect to make a career in the police service, and so 1948 saw the re-activation of the women's section as the Southern Rhodesia Women's Police Service (SRWPS). As with the men, recruitment was mainly from the United Kingdom; many of the young women who joined had served in London's Metropolitan Police and other British police forces. They were not content to undertake only passive administrative roles and continually applied pressure to take a full share of the day-to-day policing of Rhodesia. In this they were successful, doing so ultimately and at the same time obtaining command positions and achieving senior rank.

Plate 28. The British South Africa Police: Women's Services (1941, 1956 & 1974)

A major problem facing the Police Quartermaster at the time of the formation of the SRWPS was the provision of a suitable uniform. Not only had it to be distinctive and feminine but, because it was wartime and no one knew when supplies would again be available from overseas, in a material that was readily available in large quantities. Incredibly, the answer was found among the holdings of a supplier to a local religious order who happened to be over-supplied with bolts of grey cloth intended to make habits for African nuns. Since the blue cap band, lanyard and tie had been a popular innovation to the uniform for male members of the Force, it followed that the same distinctive blue should be reflected in the dress of the women. The resulting uniform, designed incidentally by an all-male committee, consisted of a jacket and skirt in grey worsted cloth, with pointed navy blue cuffs, similarly coloured shoulder straps and a grey cloth belt. In its first presentation, headgear was a grey field service cap with blue piping. This was replaced with a grey felt hat in October 1941. At the same time chromium-plated buttons and insignia replaced those of brass.

The uniform for the reactivated SRWPS of 1947, designed by a Rhodesian couturier, was based upon recommendations made by a Police Dress Committee. The theme of grey and blue, begun with the SRWAPS, was continued. Apart from a box-style winter jacket, some alterations to cut and the position of the hemline dictated by the vagaries of female fashion, the major change to the earlier uniform was the introduction of a navy blue cap that closely followed the air hostess style of the era.

The policewoman's uniform, in its final form and presentation, made its debut at a passing out parade in the Police Depot on 5th April 1973. It represented the logical outcome of a Board of Enquiry convened by the Commissioner of Police in January 1972—*To investigate the production of a new uniform for women police...* Two policewomen served as members of the Board and as far as was humanly possible the opinions of all serving policewomen were canvassed. The result, unfortunately, represented a triumph of fashion over practicality:

Summer Dress: a short-sleeved "A" line dress in uniform blue crimplene material— with a Pandit Nehru collar; concealed back zip opening; no pockets and worn without a lanyard. A decorative topstitched panel of four anodized gold BSAP 24-ligne buttons extended from just below the collar to the bust line concealing a pen pocket. Matching with shoes and handbag, the wet-look patent-leather navy blue detachable epaulettes bore the anodized rank badges and titles.

Winter Dress: the same as the above, but in a heavier material.

Winter Jacket: a uniform blue-coloured, long-sleeve collarless jacket, with a round neck designed to fit under the collar of the winter dress; the jacket having a button front with seven buttons to fasten. A tab ran across the sleeve, just above the cuff, with button trim that was for decorative purposes only. The jacket was fully lined to thigh length, had no pockets and was worn without lanyard.

Head Dress: a navy blue, fur-felt Robin Hood style hat with narrow gold piping cord around the seam where the crown and brim met. An embroidered cap badge was sewn to the centre-front.

Leatherwork: a wet-look, patent, dyed-through leather handbag was to accommodate handcuffs and other necessaries.

Plate 28

BSA Police Cadet

An early Police Cadet, writing for the regimental magazine, *The Outpost*, in March 1934, noted: *...our uniform is a replica of that of the police except that we have no riding kit. Our full dress consists of helmet, tunic, bandolier, shirt, puttees and boots (AP).*

The cadet uniform of the 1960s comprised: brown shoes, blue-topped stockings, khaki shorts, grey shirt worn with the blue tie and the distinctive *BSAP Cadet* embroidered on a pale blue background as a shoulder flash; a cap SD with pale blue band and regimental badge. For winter and on full dress occasions, the police whipcord tunic was worn with a cloth belt and the distinguishing shoulder flash of the type displayed on the shirt. Chrome buttons, badges and insignia were exchanged for similar gold anodized items in June 1973. The clothing issue for Cadets included a waterproof trench coat that had a cold-weather lining.

BSAP Cadet

The British South Africa Police: The Support Unit

While it could be said that the lineage of the Support Unit traced back to the Reserve Company of Angoni recruited in 1898, its history, as a separate functional unit, really began with the formation of the Askari Platoon in 1918. At that time Southern Rhodesia had no standing army and, as the fear of a native uprising was still quite pervasive, a reserve of military force was thought to be necessary.

Armed Native Police had been used successfully early in the war, and later the Rhodesia Native Regiment had earned battle honours in German East Africa, which tended to confirm the reliability of the African under arms when properly trained and led. Recruiting for the Platoon commenced among men disbanded from the RNR, many of whom were alien natives—Angonis and Nyasas—preference being given to those who had previously served with the Force. The main requirements were above-average physical attributes and an affinity with the profession of arms. The higher standard of education and the inquiring mind of the man recruited for normal police work were not, then, considered necessary.

Police Askari 1917

Afterward, although the Platoon took to the field in support of police mobile columns, showed the flag around the Colony, and did sterling work in the occasional civil unrest such as the strike at Wankie Colliery, its duties developed into little more than tours of guard duty at Governors' residences and appearance on ceremonial parades. The Platoon's relative lack of productivity in spheres of usual police activity led other sections of the Force to refer to them collectively—and somewhat unkindly—as *the Chocolate Soldiers*,[11] a description that overlooked their potential.

After the unrest and political disturbances in the latter years of Federation, it was considered that maintaining a body of men with little or no training in actual police work, simply for ceremonial purposes, was an expensive luxury. Consequently the duties of the Platoon were changed and the number of men increased to form the basis of what was to be the Support Unit. Three troops, each comprising four European NCOs and 30 African NCOs and men, were raised—two for assistance to Provinces where need dictated and one to be held in the Depot for ceremonial guards and other duties as required. Subsequently a further three troops were added to make up Troops A to F which, following the considerable expansion of later years, were to be referred to by the Unit itself as *The Old and Bold*.

11 The euphemism owing as much to skin colour as to comic opera.

Sergeant Major BSA Police Platoon 1965

Troops of the Support Unit were trained as standard riot sections, large baton parties, self-contained rural patrol units and for Government House Guards and ceremonial. Their training also provided for preventative patrolling and observation duties in instances of any epidemic of crime. When the internal security situation improved the Unit were employed on semi-permanent duties at Restriction Centres where the erstwhile political activists and thugs were lodged.

With the first terrorist incursions of 1966 the Support Unit accepted a new role in counter-guerrilla warfare. Their job was to patrol the bush to look for signs of the invader and to follow his spoor. Having located the terrorist groups the *bigger guns* of the Rhodesian Army were supposed to be called upon. More often than not, however, there was not the time for such procedure and the Unit dealt with the enemy itself. In many such encounters members of the Support Unit notched up honours that were in the best traditions of the Force. They developed a reputation for toughness and bushcraft and earned the respect of all they encountered.

The Support Unit's ceremonial and other extraneous duties at Government House ceased upon Rhodesia's assumption of Independence, but were resumed when the Officer Administering the Government, the Honourable Mr Clifford Dupont (later the first President of the Republic of Rhodesia) took up residence.

Terrorist attacks intensified in December 1972 and escalated to full-scale war operations when the Portuguese retreated from their African possessions in 1974. The role of the Support Unit altered to meet the continuing threat. Increased in strength to 30 troops, plus a mounted troop, it was able, latterly, to field the equivalent of two battalions of wholly self-contained mobile infantry whose task was to seek and destroy the enemy wherever he might be found.

Identifying its military role, the BSA Police Support Unit adopted a crest and shoulder-flashes that portrayed a Martial Eagle about to strike, together with the motto *Pamberi ne Gondo*, meaning *to the front with the eagle*. The Unit also adopted as its marching-song, an adaptation of the Shona war song *Mai Mababa* (My Father and Mother):

> *Going away to the Hondo* [war]
> *If I die, do not cry for me*
> *because I die for you.*

The Support Unit, the old Platoon, rejoiced in other nicknames other than *the Chocolate Soldiers. Super Police* and *Key men of the Valley* were but two jingoistic superlatives applied by the media—but the proudest name of all was *Black Boot*[12].

To a *Black Boot* only one thing was as good as he—and that was another *Black Boot*.

12 This 'unofficial' title of the Unit derived from the distinctive black leather-work of its full dress uniform.

Plate 29. The British South Africa Police Support Unit: Constable 1974

The Askari of the original Police Platoon was issued with a similar scale of clothing to that received by the District Native Police of the period, with additional items of distinction being, of first importance in the matter of prestige, his boots, and then, functionally, the web equipment:

Boots, Brown, AP pr: 2	*Knickers, Khaki-drill: 3*
Cap, Askari: 2	*Puttees, Khaki (SC) pr: 4*
Coat, GI Khaki: 1	*Shirt, Grey: 2*
Jersey, Blue: 1	*Tunic, Full Dress: 1*
Jumper, Khaki-drill: 2	*Web-equipment, Set: 1*

The web equipment issued at that time was the British Army pattern of 1908. An entrenching tool handle was held by web attachments to the bayonet frog.

Full Dress assumed after World War II and worn for the Royal Visit of 1947 and afterward until 1969, consisted of heavily starched, open-necked long-sleeved khaki drill tunic and shorts, plus khaki puttees worn with blue hose-tops; distinctive black leather-work and the dark blue-black fez with its gold tassel (the latter a feature of full dress shared only with the Regimental Band). Depot training dress comprised the trousers of Riot Kit, topped by a grey shirt. Rural patrolling and security duties were performed in full (blue) Riot Kit.

The Constable illustrated is a member of G Troop, the ceremonial troop, wearing full-dress parade order.

G Troop, using military parlance might be referred to as *the invalids*, being composed of war-wounded and light duty men. Very rarely was this dress order worn by men of the operational troops of the Unit who were issued with a full scale of combat clothing of the type (shown later) worn by members of PATU.[13] The web equipment worn was a locally manufactured version[14] of the then current NATO pattern, adapted to suit Rhodesian conditions.

13 Police Anti-Terrorist Unit(s)
14 So much for sanctions!

Shoulder Flash BSAP Support Unit

Plate 29

Plate 30. The British South Africa Police: Patrol Officer (Motor Cycle Escort Duty) 1976

The September 1927 issue of *The Outpost* published as a leader-page item the first official photograph of members of the BSAP mounted upon the eight 350cc BSA motor cycles that had been acquired for test purposes two months earlier. The members concerned appear to be dressed for a full dress occasion as they are seen to be wearing the No. 1 Dress of the day comprising: a Universal Helmet; stand up collar khaki-drill tunic; bandolier MI; Bedford cord pantaloons; khaki puttees; brown "Southall" boots and—incongruously—spurs!

Traffic sections of the Town Police came into existence in 1929. A painting by Diana Mallet-Veale[15] (c. 1941) portrays *Constable Motor Cyclist* more appropriately dressed to the Town Police scale in khaki forage cap with white cap-cover and goggles; khaki-drill tunic with numerals on a stand-up collar; whistle-chain (attached to the base of the collar); pantaloons BC (breeches), and motor cycle gauntlets. A khaki-green gabardine tunic would have been worn as full dress.

15 Early Rhodesian water-colourist and wife of Trooper Mallet Veale (BSACP).

Constable Motor Cyclist 1941

The Patrol Officer illustrated is wearing No. 1 Dress of the BSAP, worn by members of the Force performing motor cycle escort duties. The dress order is:

Belt and Brace	*Lanyard, whistle, blue*
Boots, brown	*Leggings*
Breeches (Pantaloons BC)	*Pouch, ammunition, leather*
Case, pistol, leather	*Shirt, drab*
Gauntlets, escort	*Tie, blue*
Helmet, motor cycle	*Tunic, full dress, whipcord*
Lanyard, pistol, blue	*Whistle*
Medals.	

With variations in headgear and appointments, Dress Order No. 1 was worn for Mounted Escort duties: motor cycle duties in cold weather and for ceremonial parades and other special occasions when ordered.

The medal worn in this instance is the Rhodesia General Service Medal.

Crash helmets became general issue for motor cycle duties in 1961. These were then of the cork-lined pattern at that time worn by London's Metropolitan Police. The locally manufactured fibreglass helmet was first issued to Traffic Sections in 1975 and became part of the basic scale of issue shortly thereafter. The high-gloss helmet badge was displayed on the crash helmet only when the member wearing it was engaged on ceremonial escort duties.

Plate 30

The Regimental Band of the British South Africa Police

As was the case with much of early Rhodesian history, little was recorded about military bands. It is known that the Rhodesia Horse had a band in Salisbury, under the direction of Bandmaster C.W. Day, and that it was from this source that musicians were drawn to form the first Regimental Band of the British South Africa Police in 1896. It is noteworthy that in 1897 the Force was able to field bands to play at Queen Victoria's Diamond Jubilee celebrations, both in Bulawayo and Salisbury.

By 1900 the Band was flourishing. Photographs taken in that year show a band of 25 musicians in Salisbury, under the baton of Bandmaster J. Hinds, and a band of similar proportions in Bulawayo under the direction of Bandmaster T. Scott and Trumpet Sergeant-Major J.F. Mee.

Regrettably, official interest in police bands waned and by 1910 they had ceased to exist. Nevertheless, many members appear to have maintained an interest by performing with the band of the Southern Rhodesia Volunteers. It was not until 1930 that the Force enjoyed the services of its own band again, when Trumpet Sergeant-Major Harding assembled a drum and fife band from amongst trumpeters under his supervision. Drum and fife bands have their limitations, however, and so shortly before the Second World War steps were taken to equip a full military band. Potential bandsmen were selected from serving African members of the Force who commenced training under Sergeant Max Sparks in November 1939.

Sergeant Sparks worked a positive miracle with the very raw material he had to hand. Musical notation, for example, was taught by an association with the differing denominations of local currency[16]. The new band gave its first public performance in September 1940 taking part in celebrations to commemorate the Golden Jubilee of the arrival in Salisbury of the Pioneer Column.

Soon the Band was in demand throughout the Colony and elsewhere. During 1943 it paid a goodwill visit to Beira in Portuguese East Africa. After the war, visits were made to Northern Rhodesia and to Bechuanaland where, in Lobatsi, members of the Band had the honour to be presented to His Majesty, King George VI. Later the Band was to figure prominently in the Royal Tour of 1947.

For his services to music, Superintendent Sparks was awarded the MBE in 1963.

Superintendent Sparks retired as Director of Music in November 1965 and was succeeded by Chief Inspector K.W. Barnfield, a Knellar Hall trained military bandmaster of the old school. Barnfield moulded what was until then a somewhat heterogeneous ensemble into a truly military band. He retired in June 1970 handing over the baton to Inspector D. Tasker who was later to assume the title Director of Music. Under its Bandmaster/Director of Music, the Band was to achieve a strength of

16 Pounds, shillings and pence.

two Assistant Bandmasters, an Instructing Percussionist and 65 or more attested musicians.[17]

Notwithstanding the presence of other military band organizations in the country, the Regimental Band of the British South Africa Police may truly be said to have been the National Band of Rhodesia.

Kum-A-Kye, a local adaptation of a folk song from the American West, was accepted as the Regimental March of the BSAP on 5th July 1941. Prior to this the Police had marched on and off parade to the tune of *The British Grenadiers*. The march *Rhodesians Bold*, composed after the Mashona rebellion by Charles Warren Day to honour the policemen of that time was, from August 1970, adopted as the Quick March of the Force to follow immediately upon *Kum-A-Kye*.

---

17 A Drum and Fife Band was contemplated for the Force military wing—the BSA Police Support Unit.

Band Full Dress Tunic (circa 1951)

Plate 31. The British South Africa Police Band: Drum Major 1978

Dress Orders for the first Regimental Band of the British South Africa Police were much the same as those for the (District) Mounted Police of the era. Photographic record suggests that khaki-drill was more often worn in those early days, with Full Blues being reserved for the formal occasion and ceremonial. In the 1930s the uniforms of Trumpet Sergeant-Major Harding's 20-man ensemble similarly matched those of Native Town Policemen.

Because of the economic exigencies of war, considerable ingenuity had to be employed to produce the uniforms for the new military band before it made its first appearance in September 1940. A newspaper of the day described bandsmen as *presenting an imposing appearance*—in the following:

> *Khaki-drill tunic worn with regimental badges on a stand-up collar, fastened with hooks and eyes. Dark blue shoulder straps with small regimental buttons at the point. Five medium buttons down the front and small buttons fastening the breast pockets. Khaki-drill shorts. S fastening black leather belt bearing on the right side a black leather music pouch embellished with the regimental badge. Black fez with regimental badge at the front and gold tassel hanging over the left shoulder. Black boots, black puttees with blue hose tops.*[18]

It was agreed by the Band Committee that while this uniform *was ...quite adequate in circumstances of war, the development of a distinctive full-dress for the band [was] to be given consideration at the earliest opportunity.*

Band Committee Minute No 488 of 26th June 1946 records that the following uniform was approved:

- *(a)* *Dark blue fez with blue and gold tassel and fire-gilt regimental buttons.*
- *(b)* *Dark blue tunic and trousers with ¼ inch old gold piping around the base of the collar and cuffs and down the side seams of the trousers, and fire-gilt regimental buttons.*
- *(c)* *Belt—similar to the type used by the Royal Artillery—of woven material in blue and gold, to be fastened at the left side with a toggle.*
- *(d)* *Black boots.*

It was this uniform that the band wore for duties connected with the Royal Tour of 1947.

In 1951 the full dress uniform for bandsmen was changed to provide for:

- *(i)* *Double narrow gold stripes on the trousers;*
- *(ii)* *gold wire shoulder cords;*

18 Uniform Book circa 1940.

(iii) *a gold tassel replacing that of blue and gold;*

(iv) *gold ribbon facings: around the collar, with regimental badges on black backing plates, and in seven bars across the chest fastened with small buttons at the points;*

(v) *½ inch gold ribbon on the belt in three stripes, and to form Austrian knots on the cuffs.*

In the next decade this uniform underwent subtle changes that eventually saw the eradication of the facing braid and its replacement by yellow oak-leaf cotton braid at the collar and on the belt.

The author had the privilege of designing the uniform, portrayed in the illustration, that was issued in December 1977. The idea for the design came from an old "Red-Coat" uniform worn by the 1st City of London Regiment, Royal Fusiliers in 1890. It is faced throughout with half-inch gold chevron lace, set off to advantage by high-gloss regimental badges.[19]

The Drum Major's mace and sash were presented to the Regiment in June 1961. The sash was replaced in August 1971 by the item illustrated.

Photographic record indicates that when the Police Band was touring beyond Rhodesia's borders, Sergeant Sparks had affected a white naval-type uniform which, in itself, was quite striking. However, this particular uniform did not survive. From the Band's formation, in 1940, the Dress Order for Bandmasters in ceremonial and other formal occasions consisted of a blue Colonial Police pattern cap, jacket and trousers worn with a blue shirt, black tie and shoes. A distinctive ceremonial uniform for the Director of Music, also designed by the author, was issued in December 1977 to complement the new uniform worn by bandsmen. This was based upon the frock worn by the Director of Music of the Coldstream Guards, but in "police" blue.

---

19 The fez and tassel were replaced by the British Army Bandsman Shako with gold over blue pom pom (which of themselves represented the re-introduction of nineteenth century clothing items) when the band became the Band of the Zimbabwe Republic Police in 1982.

R. HAMLEY '99

Plate 31

The British South Africa Police Reserve

While the services of a limited number of *Specials*, former members of the Force or men with previous police experience, were utilized during the First World War, no effort was made to form a standing reserve of police in Rhodesia until the mid-1920s. The Defence Act No 23 of 1926 gave the Governor of Southern Rhodesia powers to establish for the BSAP a Police Reserve and a Field Reserve; the former a force which could be called upon to serve with the regular force both within and outside the colony, and the latter for use only within the confines of Southern Rhodesia in times of national emergency.

However, it was not until the onset of the Second World War that these powers were given effect and a Reserve created. The intentions of 1926 were changed somewhat by the creation of two sections of the Reserve—referred to as the First and Second Reserve. The First Reserve was comprised of members with previous police or military experience who attested for continuous war service, and consisted of mounted and dismounted branches that were uniformed and equipped, but not paid. The Second Reserve, who were not issued with uniforms or equipment, were to be called upon to help police in times of emergency.

In July 1941, the Southern Rhodesia Women's Auxiliary Police Service came into existence. Like the Police Reserve, the formation of SRWAPS was intended to release regular members of the Force for active military duty. Had it not been for the services of the men and women of the citizens' volunteer force of the Police Reserve, the regular force, reduced in wartime to a skeletal structure, could not have carried on.

At the end of the war the Police Reserve were stood down; but faced with the prospect of racial conflict of the kind that was infecting the rest of Africa, it was decided to reinstate it. By 1954 a pattern of Reserve training had emerged which allowed for the immediate call-out of a large body of European Reservists, well prepared to deal with the kind of eventuality that had occurred to the north.

In the ensuing years the Reserve grew and training improved and broadened in scope. When the test came in the early 1960s, the Reserve was ready to meet it. Realizing, perhaps for the first time, that a breakdown of law and order would affect their own businesses, homes and loved ones, Africans clamoured to be allowed to join in order to participate in their own protection. The result was that in the event of future unrest troublemakers were to be faced with a police force that could double or treble its strength in a matter of hours.

In the larger centres members of the "A" Reserve carried out voluntary duties that included working in charge offices, traffic sections and at suburban stations. The services of the Police Reserve Airwing, a band of volunteer airmen who put themselves and their aircraft at the disposal of police in support of criminal investigations, searches and operational duties, likewise proved invaluable.

The first terrorist incursions occurred in 1966 and, with something of a lull in 1969, continued until 1970. During this period the Reserve with the Regular Force, adapted to the new situation by forming Police Anti-Terrorist Units (PATU), cheerfully undertaking border patrols under very difficult conditions. The Women's Section of the "A" reserve was established in 1971.

The latter part of 1972 saw the resumption of terrorist activity that intensified in 1975 with the granting of independence to Mozambique.

The Police Special Reserve, supplementing the contribution of the General Reserve to the policing of urban areas, was resuscitated in 1974. In 1975 the National Service scheme began to have an effect on reserve services and boosted manpower considerably. This year also found African Police Reservists being utilized in a variety of active roles. A Mounted Unit was formed and deployed for counter-insurgency duties and, towards the close of the year, a Marine Division of the BSA Police Reserve commenced duty on Lake Kariba.

In its final form, the Police Reserve consisted of:

- *(1) The Police Special Reserve—made up of:*
  - *(a) Residential Special Reservists: appointed to perform patrolling duties in their own residential areas, and*
  - *(b) Key Point Special Reservists: appointed to perform duties at certain important installations.*

- *(2) The Police General Reserve—made up of:*
  - *(a) The A Reserve: composed of male and female members willing to assist the Regular Force on emergency and counter-insurgency duties and, in addition, perform a minimum of 16 hours of routine duty every month, and*
  - *(b) The Field Reserve later known as The B Reserve: composed of European male and female and African male members required to assist the Force on emergency duties whenever necessary. The B Reserve was inclusive of:*
  - *(i) The General B Reserve: Male members performing general operational and administrative duties (comprised the bulk of the Reserve).*
  - *(ii) The Police Reserve Airwing: Male and female members holding current flying licences.*
  - *(iii) The Marine Division: Members providing crews for privately owned boats, and marine technicians.*
  - *(iv) Special Branch and CID Units: Members with special skills attached to the Regular Special Branch and CID.*
  - *(v) Specialized Units: Technicians and members with special skills—armourers, radio technicians, motor mechanics, etc., and members employed in data processing, photography, finance clerks and training staff.*
  - *(vi) The Women's Field Reserve: Members employed as radio operators, transport drivers, on station administration, general police and operational duties.*
  - *(vii) The African Field Reserve: Members employed on operational and general crime prevention duties.*

(viii) Police Anti-terrorist Units (PATU): Members employed on counter-insurgency and active operational duties.

(ix) Mounted Units: Normally PATU members in rural areas using their own horses for follow-up and patrols.

(x) The Reserve of Officers: Ex-regular police officers holding the rank of Reserve Superintendent and assisting at JOCs (Joint Operations Command).

Pilot Brevet – Airwing

Plate 32. The British South Africa Police: Patrol Officer "A" Reserve

A member appointed to the BSA Police A Reserve was issued with the same items of uniform that formed the basic clothing issue for members of the regular force—in this instance: a cap (drab) with blue band and cap badge; winter dress consisting of a suit of whipcord worn either with a belt of self material fastened with an anodized buckle or a brown leather waist belt with gilt clasp and sliding buckle; a drab green shirt; blue tie; blue lanyard and whistle; rank and collar badges; brown leather shoes; khaki socks; anodized shoulder titles "BSAP" and collar titles "R". Summer dress comprised a suit (tunic and shorts) of khaki-terylene material, worn with a waist belt of leather or in self-material; blue-topped stockings and brown shoes.

A B Reservist received the same items of "riot kit" and combat clothing as were issued to Regular members of the Force (Plates 24 and 33). These items were *additional* issues to members of the A Reserve.

A member of the Women's Field Reserve was issued with a grey felt hat, grey overalls with matching belt, a blue cardigan and black shoes. Chrome cap badges, buckle, small buttons and titles "R" and "BSAP" were replaced with similar gold-anodized items in 1973. The (1941) vintage pork-pie pattern grey felt hat was heartily disliked by the ladies of the Reserve serving in later years and they were not at all unhappy when sanctions induced a shortage of fur-felt and occasioned the hat's replacement by a more fashionable adaptation of the peaked combat cap in grey material, set off with the embroidered hat badge worn by regular policewomen.

Badges of rank of members of the A Reserve had, since the branch was formed, conformed to those worn by regular members of the Force holding equivalent rank. Police General Headquarters All stations Circular No 23 of 1977, however, advised:

> *...the following rank structure and badges of rank have been approved for the Field Reserve, which hereafter will be referred to as the B Reserve:*

Rank	*Badges of Rank*	*Total number of men normally controlled*
Field Reservist	*Nil*	–
Stick Leader	*One wavy bar*	*5 men*
Section Leaders	*Two wavy bars*	*25 men*
Group Leader	*Three wavy bars*	*100 men or station total*

In regulations drafted to cover the new Police Reserve rank structure, the *wavy bar* is described as ... *a bar with alternate contrary curves...for ease of identification described as a wavy bar.*

The earlier titled "Field Reserve" had only one rank—that of Field Reservist. For purposes of discipline and administration, however, Section Leaders were appointed by Members-in-Charge Stations or Provincial (Police Reserve) Inspectors, and were identified by distinctive flashes worn on the shoulder straps of their blue or camouflaged jackets.

The Special Reserve—affectionately referred to as *Wombles*[20]—were issued with a more economically produced blue "boiler suit", worn with brown boots and a fibreglass riot helmet.

20 Animalistic characters portrayed on British Television in the 1970s in support of current environmental issues.

Plate 32

Plate 33. The British South Africa Police: Patrol Officer (PATU Duties) 1978

The outfit worn by the Patrol Officer in this illustration represents the basic camouflaged clothing and equipment that was developed to meet bush warfare conditions in Rhodesia. Such items were worn by members of the Support Unit, the Mounted Unit and by all members of the Force engaged upon anti-terrorist and counter-insurgency operations in other than urban situations.

The weapon carried is a 7,62 FN Light Automatic Rifle which was received by the BSAP in 1962.

Earlier, when meeting the first terrorist incursions, Police were obliged to take to the field wearing *emergency and musketry dress* or *riot kit*, as it was known. However, as the combination of light grey shirts and blue trousers tended to make members stand out from the surrounding bush like the proverbial sore thumb, a rapid change-over to military camouflage clothing was called for.

First to be issued, in 1967, were smocks made up in a camouflaged mercerized twill material, similar in style and design to that worn by British Airborne Forces in the latter part of World War II, together with jungle-green denim trousers and twill material shirts as then worn by the Rhodesian Army. Combat Kit proper came *on-stream* in the early part of 1968. As first conceived it consisted of a cap with neck protector, made up in camouflaged twill material; long-sleeved *jungle green* twill shirts; camouflaged denim trousers; khaki-green short canvas gaiters, and brown leather boots having either poro-crepe or *vibram* soles. Webbing at that time was up-dated 1944 pattern equipment and was used together with a heavy-duty framed rucksack designed to carry, in addition to a change of clothing, several days' rations, a poncho cape, sleeping bag and extra ammunition. In 1969 the drab green shirt was replaced by a shirt of camouflaged twill material; the boots and gaiters, as time progressed, by custom-made combat boots with Swiss uppers; and the webbing by a local development of the then current NATO[21] equipment.

Over the years experience showed that the combat cap offered less protection from the Rhodesian sun than did the previously issued soft jungle hat. Increasingly preference was given to the issue of the older pattern headgear.[22]

Permitted free reign to his own eccentricities of dress under active service conditions, the younger Rhodesian soldier and policeman would be seen to wear the minimum of clothing consisting of little more than a cap or soft hat, a shirt with no sleeves or a T-shirt, shorts and *veldschoens*[23] or hockey boots—considering anything else, other than his weapon of choice, an unnecessary encumbrance.

---

21 North Atlantic Treaty Organization.
22 Sometimes referred to as "Hats, Floppy & Ridiculous".
23 A South African boot/shoe of untanned hide.

Cloth badges of rank that slipped on to the epaulettes of the shirt or combat jacket, served to identify members of the BSAP when engaged in counter-insurgency duties. Central Planning Committee minute No 7 of 1973 gave approval for active members of PATU to wear the identifying leopard pug shoulder flash and for the Support unit to wear as their peculiar unit insignia a shoulder flash portraying a bird of prey design.

Urban terrorism required a different response from that supplied by PATU. Police Urban Emergency Units were introduced, experimentally, in Bulawayo in 1975—and as they proved successful—in Salisbury and Umtali also in 1976. More readily recognized by the television appellation *SWAT*[24], the BSAP Urban Emergency Units were made up of members of the Regular Force—especially trained to combat urban terrorism, hostage situations, aircraft hijacking, and the entire range of armed and dangerous criminality.

Each unit consisted of two or more teams of nine men plus a Woman Patrol Officer who had the responsibility of searching and guarding female prisoners and for rendering first aid when required. Teams were as lightly equipped as possible and armed from their own resources, as the situation dictated. Their basic clothing and equipment was listed as:

Helmet (NATO pattern)—painted a matt dark blue; Cap peaked, blue (baseball type); Overalls, combination, blue; Boots, black (SAS pattern- hockey type); Belt, web, blue; Holster, web, blue; Pouch, web, blue; Respirator; Waistcoat, combat (with pockets for magazines, grenades, maps, radio and field dressings, loops for shotgun cartridges, and a large pocket at the rear to accommodate a poncho—the jacket zipped at the front and with shoulder padding); Body Armour.

Following bombing incidents in the City of Salisbury in 1977, police Cordon and Search exercises were initiated on a daily basis. Composed, in the main, of Urban Field Reserve under the direction of regular members of the Force, Cordon & Search Teams wore Dress Order No 5—Emergency and Musketry Dress.

---

24 ie. Special Weapons & Tactics

7.62 mm FN Light Automatic Rifle and Shoulder Flash – PATU

Plate 33

ON 3RD MARCH 1978, an internal settlement was arranged among the warring internal black factions and the white-led Government. Early the following year, on 30th January 1979, Rhodesia's white population accepted a majority-rule constitution at referendum. In April there were *One man-one vote* elections that, with the BSAP providing security, were universally accepted as being both free and fair. These, in June, led to the formation of the first black-dominated Government of Zimbabwe/Rhodesia. Following the August 1979 Commonwealth Conference the interminable Lancaster House talks began that, in the fullness of time, were to lead to the end of Mr Smith's rebellion.

On 12th December 1979, Lord Soames arrived to assume the title of Governor. This gentleman, incidentally, did not endear himself to senior elements of the Force by his disdainful attitude toward Corps traditions and his disregard for mess etiquette. In return, and in direct contrast to his predecessor, he was regarded as a pompous ass.

On 2nd December 1979, a settlement agreement among all opposing forces was signed in London, exactly seven years after the terrorist war had begun in earnest.

Throughout these troubled times the BSAP had been fully extended in fulfilling its role in the field of law enforcement, while at the same time maintaining a substantial contribution to the security effort. The criminal element, many of whom had posed as terrorists in the commission of crimes, had been quick to take advantage of the situation. It is to the everlasting credit of the BSAP—the Regular Police, National Servicemen, Reserves, Auxiliaries and Specials—and in the best traditions of the Force, that this dual effort was sustained at so consistently high a level.

There was yet further irony in the fact that Soames's new government had to call upon the Rhodesian Security Forces to prevent hundreds of erstwhile guerrillas crossing its territorial borders in violation of the Lancaster House agreement. More irony in the fact that the BSA Police Support Unit was called upon to provide guards for the Commonwealth forces and police monitoring the cease-fire and the subsequent elections (where, helplessly, they were to observe the latter's inability to recognize native techniques in intimidation).

Independence for Zimbabwe came in 1980 and, as was to be expected, with independence came the elimination of all the appurtenances of power of the white regime. At dusk on the evening of Friday 1st August 1980, the BSA Police Flag was hauled down for the last time from the masthead at Police Headquarters (in the newly re-christened City of Harare) and folded with quiet dignity. At midnight and with no other official ceremony, that which was regarded by many as the finest police force in the world, ceased to exist.

Both as police and as soldiers, from the days of horseback in the African veldt to helicopters in a modern bush war, the BSAP fashioned a noble heritage and a great tradition that lives on gloriously in the pages of recent history and in the hearts of all former Rhodesians.

Proudly did the British South Africa Police live up to the pledge:

Pro Rege, Pro Lege, Pro Patria.

Rudyard Kipling's verse provides a fitting eulogy.

We broke a king
and we built a road.
A Court house stands where the
Regiment goed.

End Plate – Patrol Officer – Mounted Unit 1980.

Some sources and references

Frontier Patrols. Lt-Col Colin Harding: Simkin Marshall, London, 1937 [via Hickman].

Men Who Made Rhodesia. Col Selwyn Hickman: BSA Company, Salisbury, 1960 [via Hickman].

Rhodesia Served the Queen. Col Selwyn Hickman: The Government Printer, Salisbury, 1970 [via Hickman].

The First Line of Defence. Peter Gibbs: BSA Police Board of Trustees [via Mardon Press], Salisbury, Rhodesia, 1974.

The Right of the Line. Peter Gibbs: Kingston's Limited for the BSA Police Board of Trustees, Salisbury, Rhodesia, 1974.

The Times History of the War in South Africa. L.S. Amery (Ed): *The Times*, London.

The Widows Party. Rudyard Kipling.

From BSA Police Headquarters Records—Annual Reports various.

From the files of *The Outpost* (The Regimental Magazine of the British South Africa Police)—BSA Police Printers, for the BSA Police Board of Trustees, Salisbury, Rhodesia. Dates various:

The Genesis of the BSA Police. John Crawford (Sergeant 'F' Troop BBP).

Some Reminiscences of the Pioneer Expedition. C.H. Divine (Corporal 'D' Troop BSACP).

History of the BSAP Wilfred W. Bussey (Editor of the *Police Review*) [via *The Outpost* (1940)].

The South African War. A.J. Tomlinson (Trooper, Mashonaland Mounted Police).

Outpost Magazines—articles, notes and photographs of various dates to January 1981—courtesy the Editor.

An Album–Commemorating the Review of the British South Africa Police by Her Majesty Queen Elizabeth the Queen Mother, Honorary Commissioner, at Salisbury on 30th May 1960. Rhodesian Printers Limited for the BSA Police Central Fund. Salisbury, Southern Rhodesia, 1960.

Kum-a-kye. Sleeve notes—recording of The Band of the British South Africa Police—by The Brigadiers Company, Salisbury, Southern Rhodesia.

Rhodesia Calls Magazine. Salisbury, Rhodesia May – June Edition, 1965.

Encyclopaedia Rhodesia. The College Press, Salisbury, Rhodesia, 1973.

Artefacts and photographs derived from The National Archives and the Queen Victoria Museum, Salisbury, Rhodesia and from the author's personal collection.

Welcome to Covos Day Books

Southern Africa's newest publishing house

In late 1997, in Johannesburg, Covos Day Books began life as a part-time, "mailorder-from-home" business—with one title. We soon appreciate that the southern African market was not being adequately serviced in terms of non-fiction—military, historical and socio-political material. In a shor space of time, we have established ourselves as a leading African publisher in these fields. This year, 2000, we publish 14 new titles. For 2001 we have publishing schedule in place for 20 new titles. We are now expanding into international markets and our books are being enthusiastically received.

To date, our focus has been the Anglo-Boer War and the southern African "bush wars" of the 1970s and 1980s. However, we are also be developin other categories, including southern African fiction, literature and auto/biography. Without losing sight of our core business, we are, however, nc afraid to explore other diverse and exciting areas—from war poetry—to accounts of Japanese POWs in World War II—and ANC exiles during th Apartheid era. In 2001 we shall also be launching an exciting Children's Books series.

The publishing business in Africa is alive and well—producing top quality books that are vibrant, entertaining and historically relevant. Keep an e out for our titles!

- Prices indicated are recommended retail prices in South Africa, United Kingdom, USA, Canada, Australia and New Zealand.
- Prices may vary slightly and are subject to change without notice.
- Book specifications and publication dates are, in some instances, provisional.

COVOS DAY BOOKS
P. O. Box 6996
Weltevredenpark, 1715
South Africa
tel +2711-475 0922
fax +2711-475 8974
email: covos@global.co.za
website at www.mazoe.com

UK Sales and Distribution
VERULAM PUBLISHING
152a Park Street Lane, Park Street
St Albans, Herts AL2 2AU
tel +44-1727-872 770
fax +44-1727-873 886
email: verulampub@compuserve.com

USA Sales and Distribution
BHB International, Inc.
108 East North 1st Street
Suite G
Seneca, SC 29678
tel +1-864-885 9444
fax +1-864-885 1090
email: BHBBooks@aol.com

Canadian Sales and Distribution
Vanwell Publishing Limited
P.O. Box 2131
1 Northrup Crescent
St. Catherines
Ont L2R 7S2
tel +1-905-937 310
fax +1-905-937 1760
email: simon.kooter@vanwell.com

Adult Fiction

CYCLONE BLUES

Chris Cocks

The author's first novel after his best-selling nonfiction *Fireforce* and *Survival Course.* Set in present-day Zimbabwe and Mozambique, still suffering from the hangovers of civil war and natural disasters—it is a story of love and tragedy, against the backdrop of political machinations and treachery. It successfully examines inter-racial relationships and attitudes and breathes hope into a troubled sub-continent, struggling with its history, its present and its future.

Softback	222 x 152mm	294 pages	0 620 25438 6		
R74.95	£9.95	US$17.50	C$25.00	A$25.00	NZ$32.50

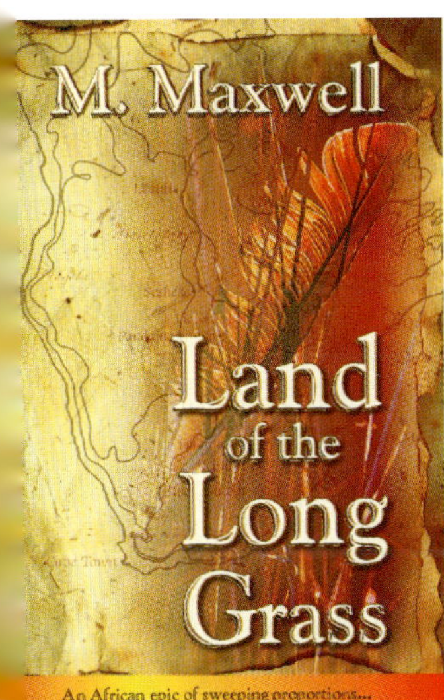

LAND OF THE LONG GRASS

M. Maxwell

A sweeping epic, based on the true story of Harrison Clark, who after fighting the Frontier wars of the Eastern Cape and Basutoland in the mid-1800s, flees to the area north of the Zambezi, where he sets himself up as Chief Changa-Changa covering a vast fiefdom. A blockbuster adventure story of love, revenge, slavery, missionaries and witchcraft.

Softback	222 x 152mm	approx 450 pages	map	0 620 26087 4	
R95.00	£10.00	US$17.50	C$25.00	A$25.00	NZ$32.50

SAND IN THE WIND

Keith Meadows

Of wildlife and war, this haunting novel, drawn from factual events and set in the great Zambezi Valley encompasses the fading era of Rhodesia to the dawn of Zimbabwe. Evocatively captures the essence of wild Africa. Following the traditions of Robert Ruark.

"A land without animals is a dead land" – Old Shangaan saying

Softback	222 x 148mm	522 pages	0 797 41785 0	Thorntree Press	
R120.00	£15.00	US$25.00	C$35.00	A$35.00	NZ$45.00

Anglo-Boer War

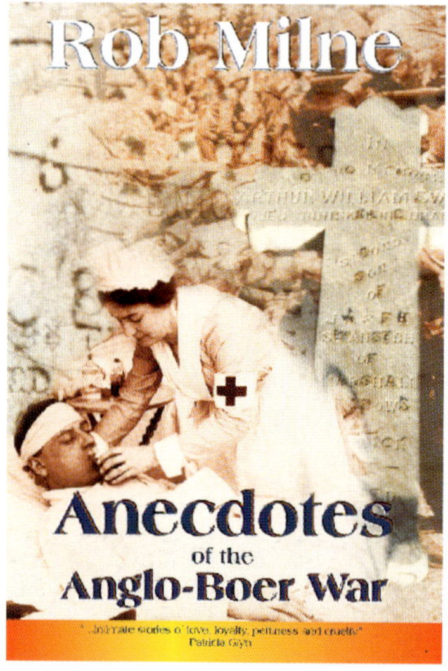

ANECDOTES OF THE ANGLO-BOER WAR

NEW August 200

Rob Milne

An absorbing collection of true stories from the Anglo-Boer War—some tragic, some light-hearted—but at all times entertaining, bringing humanity to the horror of war.

Softback	222 x 152mm	196 pages	95 b/w photographs	map	0 620 25439 4
R95.00	£10.00	US$17.50	C$25.00	A$25.00	NZ$32.5

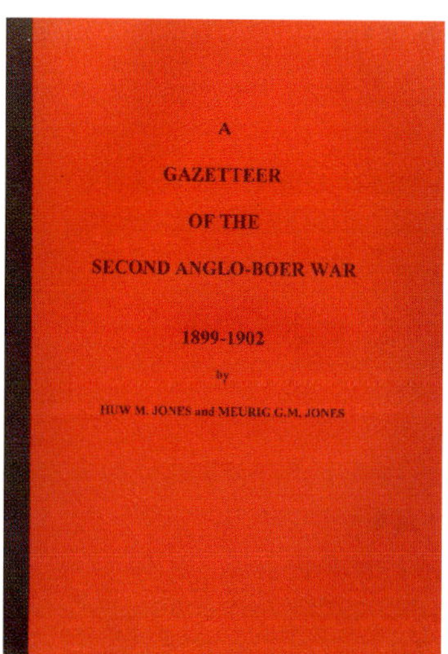

A GAZETTEER OF THE SECOND ANGLO-BOER WAR

August 200

Huw M.Jones and Meurig G.M.Jones

A comprehensive work that draws from Afrikaans, Dutch and English sources and archives, the authors have spent many yea of painstaking research compiling this encyclopaedia of events, locations and units of the Boer War. Absolutely essential reading for anyone with a passing interest, or more, in the South Africa of a century ago.

Softback	297 x 210mm	312 pages	9 maps	0 85420 175 0	The Military Pre 1999
R495.00	£50.00	US$75.00	C$125.00	A$125.00	NZ$175.0

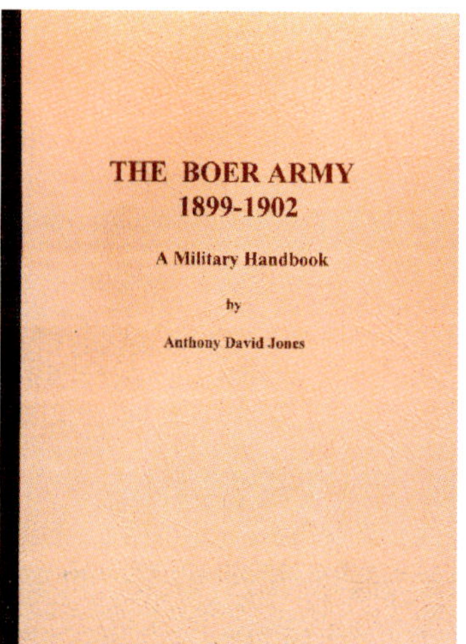

THE BOER ARMY 1899-1902 – A MILITARY HANDBOOK

Anthony David Jones

The first detailed description of the Boer forces to appear in English since the actual war 100 years ago. Includes the Transva and Orange Free State Commando structures and Order of Battle, the foreign volunteer units and the Artillery. Also listed a described are the Boer weapons, dress and Commissariat. With accounts of the Boer fighting methods and the development the guerrilla tactics.

Softback	297 x 210mm	100 pages	5 illustrations map	0 85420 240 4	The Military Pr 2000
R165.00	£20.00	US$30.00	C$40.00	A$40.00	NZ$55.0

Anglo-Boer War

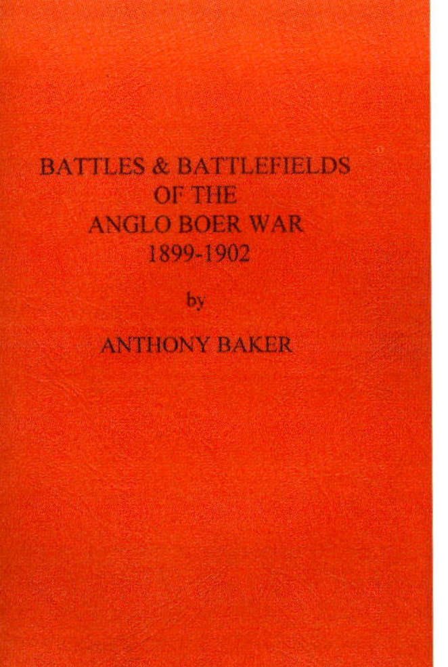

THE BATTLES AND BATTLEFIELDS OF THE ANGLO-BOER WAR 1899-1902

NEW August 2000

Anthony Baker

A must for any battlefield enthusiast, this comprehensive guide clearly and concisely outlines the significant battles that occurred. It details the dilemmas that the various commanders faced in the field on the day and how they overcame them, or didn't, with the forces they had at their disposal. With comprehensive listings of places, personalities and units.

Softback	297 x 210mm	240 pages	60 colour maps	0 85420 150 5	The Military Press 1999
R294.00	£30.00	US$50.00	C$75.00	A$75.00	NZ$100.00

VICTORIA CROSSES

of  the

Anglo-Boer War

IAN UYS

VICTORIA CROSSES OF THE ANGLO-BOER WAR

August 2000

Ian Uys

A comprehensive compilation of the stories behind the 78 VCs awarded, by one of South Africa's leading historians. We read of the two British Lions rugby players who stayed on after the 1896 tour to each win a VC, the attempted rescue of the guns at Colenso where 7 VCs were won, the blinded Scottish officer who continued leading his men and the first of the "Double VCs" to be won.

Softback	208 x 148mm	140 pages	104 illustrations	0 620 25447 5	Fortress Books 2000
R100.00	£10.00	US$17.50	C$25.00	A$25.00	NZ$32.50

BOMBARDMENT OF LADYSMITH ANTICIPATED

– The Diary of a Siege

Alan Chalmers

Into the cauldron of the siege of Ladysmith arrived the slight, Chaplinesque figure of George Maidment, a British Army orderly, fresh out from the Midlands of England. For over 100 days he recorded the events of the siege in his diary—the daily tedium, the fighting, the sniping, the lack of food, the disgust at eating their own horses. One bungled relief attempt after another as the great British Army was put through its paces by a bunch of farmers. This is a story of great courage lying alongside great stupidity, of world events alongside the personal, intimate observations of a local boy.

"Of the myriad books published for the Anglo-Boer War Centenary this is one of the best illustrated and most well written"
– Meurig Jones, Chairman, Victorian Military Society

Softback	222 x 152mm	340 pages	298 b/w illustrations	9 pullout maps	0 620 24996 X
R140.00	£15.00	US$25.00	C$35.00	A$35.00	NZ$45.00

Anglo-Boer War

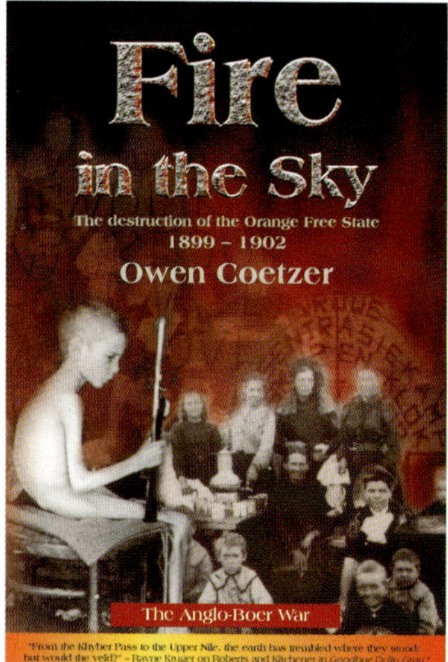

FIRE IN THE SKY – The Destruction of the Orange Free State 1899-1902

Owen Coetzer

A shocking account of Britain's official Boer War policy of scorched earth, farm burning and concentration camps. "More than 27,000 people", mainly women and children, died in appalling conditions. It was a mistake, Milner later wrote. But a brutal one, the consequences of which are still felt today. An in-depth, horrifying exposé.

Softback	222 x 152mm	362 pages	49 b/w photographs	map	0 620 24114 4
R120.00	£15.00	US$25.00	C$35.00	A$35.00	NZ$45.00

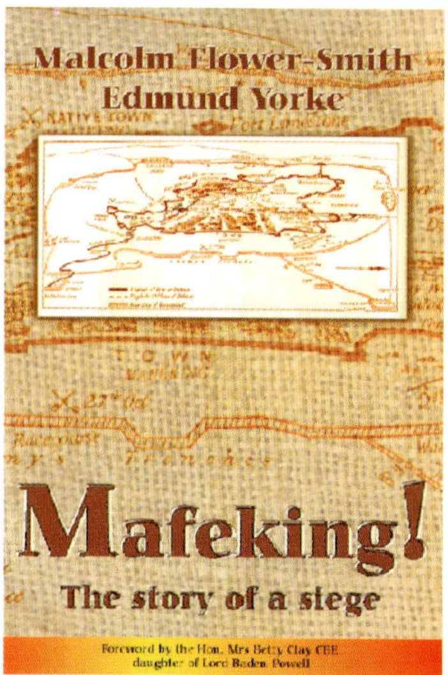

MAFEKING!

Malcolm Flower-Smith and Edmund Yorke

Psychologically affected by the fact that it was from Mafeking that the Jameson Raid was launched, the Boers determined to regain this key town. The exceptional military leadership, indomitable spirit and personal charisma of Colonel Baden-Powell made him the ideal officer for the British defence—the source of inspiration for the defenders of Mafeking during the epic 7 month siege. By March 1900, the garrison was famished; death and destruction had become daily fare. When, in May, Mafeking was finally relieved, the British nation was swept by a wave of patriotic hysteria, unequalled since.

With the foreword by The Honourable Mrs Betty Clay CBE, daughter of Lord Baden-Powell

Softback	222 x 152mm	200 pages	50 b/w illustrations	0 620 25251 0	
R100.00	£10.00	US$17.50	C$25.00	A$25.00	NZ$32.50

HOW WE KEPT THE FLAG FLYING

Donald Macdonald

Similar facsimile reprint of 1st Edition, (Ward, Lock & Co. Ltd., 1900). This enduring story of the siege of Ladysmith is the first in our series of Anglo-Boer War titles, commemorating the Anglo-Boer War Centenary 1999-2002. A classic in every sense, as relevant today as a century ago.

Hardback	213 x 137mm	303 pages	12 b/w illustrations	0 620 23342 7	2nd Edition
R100.00	£15.00	US$25.00	C$35.00	A$35.00	NZ$45.00

Anglo-Boer War

HALT! ACTION FRONT! – With Colonel Long at Colenso

Darrell Hall

The detailed account of the three batteries of the 4th Brigade Division, Royal Field Artillery (7th, 14th, and 66th), and the six "Long 12s" of the Royal Navy, which operated under the direct command of Colonel C.J. Long RHA, commanding the Artillery of the Natal Field Force, at the Battle of Colenso, on 15th December 1899. These three RFA batteries still serve today in the 26th Field Regiment, Royal Artillery, as now 16th, 17th and 159th respectively.

Hardback	228 x 155mm	208 pages	Over 100 b/w photographs	diagrams, maps	0 620 24112 8
R100.00	£15.00	US$25.00	C$35.00	A$35.00	NZ$45.00

SOUTH AFRICAN WAR BOOKS – An Illustrated Bibliography

R.G. Hackett

Definitive compilation of English language publications relating to the Anglo-Boer War 1899-1902. A masterpiece and already a collector's item, with only 1,200 copies printed.

"With meticulous regard for detail, this bibliography of contemporary books about the Boer War is a collector's must... a delightful insight into the mind of the bibliophile..." – James Mitchell, *The Star*

Hardback	316 x 222mm	216 pages	Over 200 colour & b/w illustrations	0 952 00390 2	P.G. de Lotz Military Bookseller
R850.00	£65.00	US$100.00	C$150.00	A$150.00	NZ$195.00

Auto/Biography

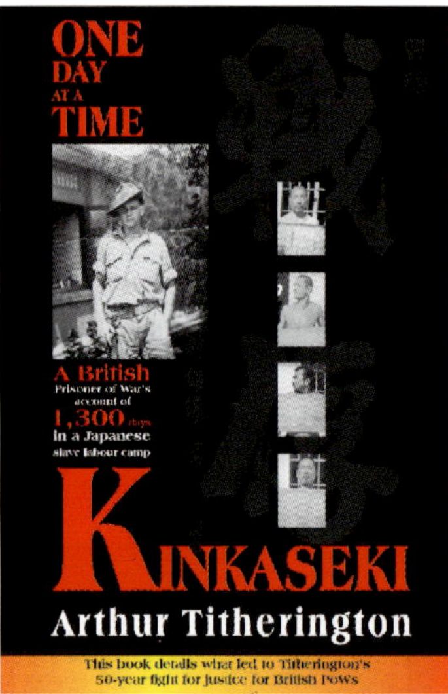

KINKASEKI – One day at a time

Arthur Titherington

Taken prisoner at the fall of Singapore, the author was to spend the rest of the war as a slave labourer in the Japanese POW camp at Kinkaseki in Formosa (now Taiwan). A chilling exposé of brutality and cruelty. A true story of survival in the tradition of *Tenko* and *The Bridge on the River Kwai.*

Softback	222 x 152mm	312 pages	50 b/w photographs	2nd Edition	0 620 25441 6
R95.00	£10.00	US$17.50	C$25.00	A$25.00	NZ$32.5

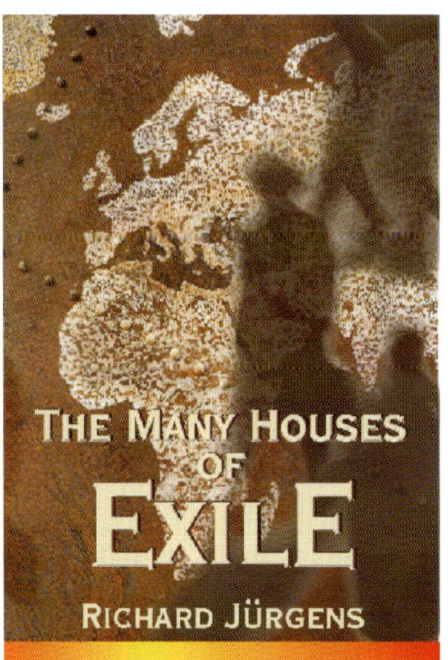

THE MANY HOUSES OF EXILE

NEW September 20

Richard Jürgens

A fascinating autobiographical account of the author's experiences as an ANC exile. From his conscription into the South Afri army, to ANC recruitment whilst studying philosophy at Wits University—to life in the ANC camps in Zambia, Tanzania and Zimbabwe—and finally to 8 years exile in Holland. Richard Jürgens is the new voice of South African literature.

Softback	222 x 152mm	486 pages	0 620 25440 8		
R95.00	£10.00	US$17.50	C$25.00	A$25.00	NZ$32.5

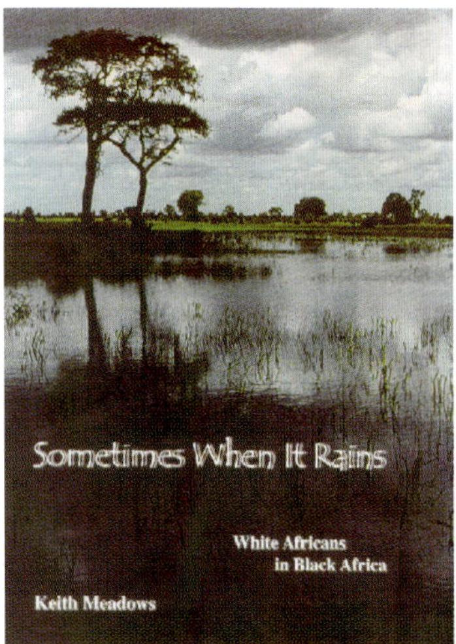

SOMETIMES WHEN IT RAINS

Keith Meadows

Colonialism has come and gone, helped on its way by African nationalism, a deep-grown chancre at last successfully lanced. Has had its just desserts in the reconstituted third world history books, being spooned in somewhere between the Spanish Inquisition and the Great Plague. But was it a legacy that barren? Here you will meet eleven ordinary people who have left their stamp on Rhodesia and subsequently Zimbabwe. Eleven white Africans who have walked that extra mile for Africa.

"...a stirring elegy to a fading way of life when character, adventure and strong opinion ruled." – John Heminway, author *African Journeys* and *No Man's Land*

Hardback	215 x 138mm	412 pages	40 b/w photographs	0 797 42135 1	Thorntree Pre 2000
R185.00	£20.00	US$35.00	C$45.00	A$45.00	NZ$60.0

Auto/Biography

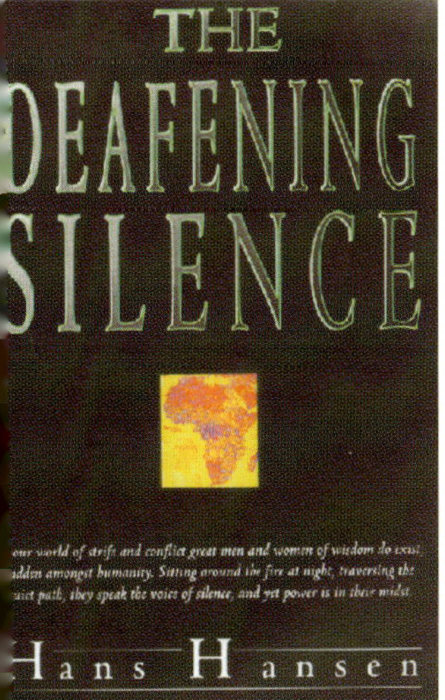

THE DEAFENING SILENCE

Hans Hansen

Far away from the safety, stability, and chill winters of his native Denmark, Hans Hansen describes the harsh reality of life in Africa. From the Kenyan Mau Mau uprising in 1952 to the Air Rhodesia Viscount Flight 827 tragedy (he was amongst the handful who survived the massacred by ZIPRA guerrillas), Hansen charts his spiritual growth alongside the violence and turbulence of Africa in a most extraordinary account.

Softback	198 x 130mm	342 pages	0 75410 189 4	Minerva Press 1998	
R145.00	£15.00	US$25.00	C$35.00	A$35.00	NZ$45.00

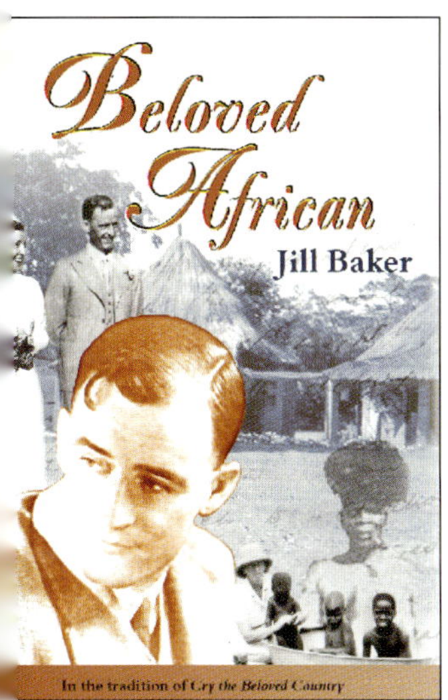

BELOVED AFRICAN

Jill Baker

The author, among Zimbabwe's, previously Rhodesia's, best-loved media personalities, writes about her enigmatic father, John Hammond, one of that country's earliest and foremost educators. A pioneer at the turn of the century, he helped forge the solid educational system that spawned some of the great minds of the country, including many of the founding black nationalists. A controversial, but much-loved figure.

In the same vein as "Cry the Beloved Country"

Hardback	228 x 155mm	508 pages	58 b/w photographs	map	0 620 24117 9
R165.00	£20.00	US$30.00	C$40.00	A$40.00	NZ$55.00

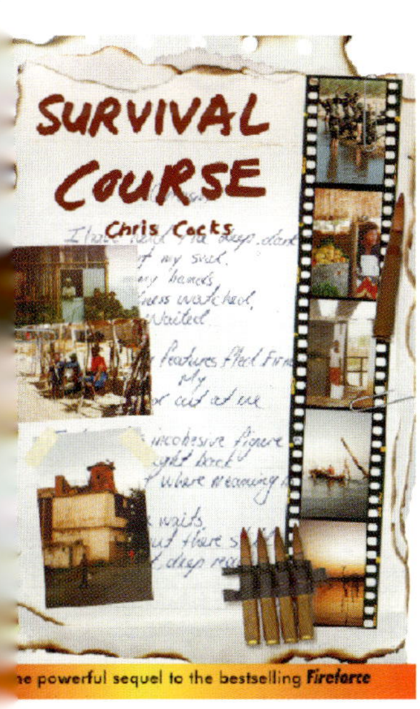

SURVIVAL COURSE

Chris Cocks

The sequel to the best-selling *Fireforce*. Chronicling the author's 15-month experience, up to Zimbabwean independence in 1980, as a stick-leader in the specialist PATU (Police Anti-Terrorist Unit), operating on Rhodesia's eastern border. Part Two of the book deals with the author's traumatic and harrowing transition to civilian life in post-war Zimbabwe.

Softback	222 x 152mm	244 pages	40 b/w photographs	map	0 620 24115 2
R95.00	£10.00	US$17.50	C$25.00	A$25.00	NZ$32.50

Auto/Biography

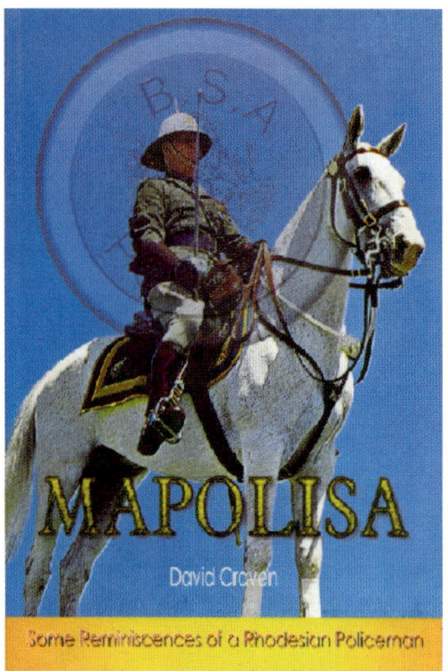

MAPOLISA – Some Reminiscences of a Rhodesian Policeman

David Craven

The author's memoirs of his service in the British South Africa Police (BSAP) 1948-69. Capturing a colonial era as "the winds change" were blowing across Africa. A delightful account of an ordinary policeman simply getting on with his job.

"...a very readable story... which needed telling" – Zimbabwe Independent

Softback	222 x 152mm	216 pages	66 b/w illustrations map	0 620 22522 X	Reprinted 2000
R100.00	£10.00	US$17.50	C$25.00	A$25.00	NZ$32.5C

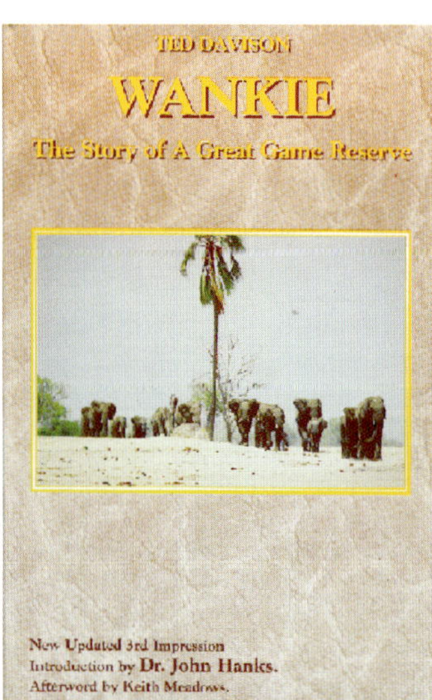

WANKIE – The Story of a Great Game Reserve

Ted Davison

The enduring account of the birth and development of one of Africa's great game reserves—the Hwange (Wankie) National Park in Zimbabwe—and the legendary ranger who started it all. With the foreword by former prime minister, Ian Douglas Smith.

"There are some who can live without wild things, and some who cannot" – Aldo Leopold, *A Sand County Almanac*

Hardback	220 x 150mm	276 pages	87 sepia illustrations sketches, maps	0 797 41874 1 3rd Impression	Thorntree Pres
R120.00	£15.00	US$25.00	C$35.00	A$35.00	NZ$45.0(

Aviation

A PRIDE OF EAGLES – The Definitive History of the Rhodesian Air Force 1920-80

NEW *November 2000*

Beryl Salt, assisted by Group Captain Bill Sykes and Wing Commander Peter Cooke

From the arrival of the *Silver Queen* in 1920, through the "Rhodesia Squadrons" of World War 2, to the cessation of hostilities after the Rhodesian bush war in 1980, the author has spent over 30 years compiling this comprehensive account of this small, but professional and effective air force. Officially endorsed by the Air Force Associations of Zimbabwe, this book will be prized by lovers of Africana and aviation buffs worldwide. Also a Special leather-bound hardback Edition.

Softback	297 x 210mm	approx 450 pages	Over 1,000 photographs	maps, diagrams	0 620 23759 7
Standard Edition R295.00	£30.00	US$50.00	C$75.00	A$75.00	NZ$100.00
Special Edition R995.00	£100.00	US$175.00	C$250.00	A$250.00	NZ$325.00

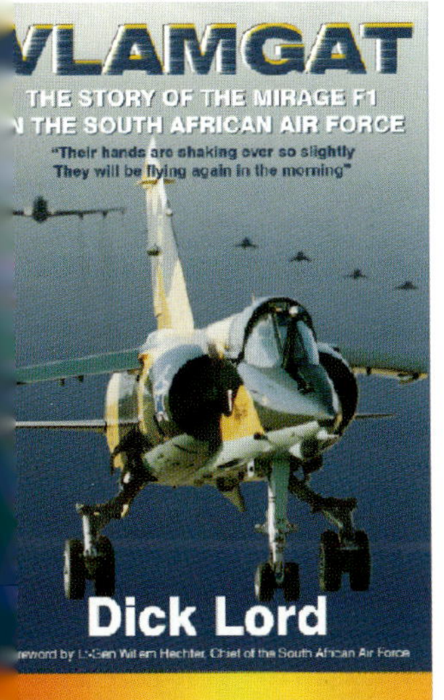

VLAMGAT – The Story of the Mirage F1 in the South Africa

Brigadier Dick Lord

The sequel to *Fire, Flood and Ice,* this is an outstanding compilation of stories and experiences of SAAF Mirage pilots who operated in the Angolan and the SWA/Namibian bush wars. The author, an ex-Top Gun and Fleet Air Arm pilot, was at one time the CO of 1 Squadron (Mirages), the SAAF. A thrilling account told "from the cockpit".

Hardback	228 x 155mm	380 pages	55 colour 169 b/w photographs	maps, diagrams	0 620 24116 0
R185.00	£20.00	US$35.00	C$45.00	A$45.00	NZ$60.00

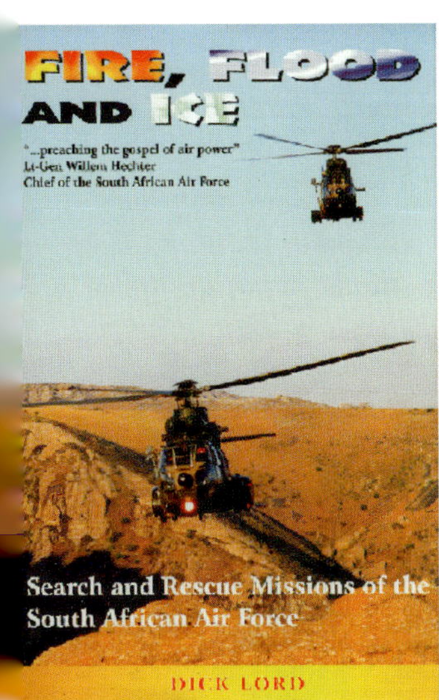

FIRE, FLOOD AND ICE – Search and Rescue Missions of the South African Air Force

Brigadier Dick Lord

A compilation of South African search and rescue missions, both military and civil, over the past decade. Foreword by Lieutenant-General Willem Hechter, Chief of the SAAF. Of heartwarming dedication and courage, these true stories will leave the reader breathless.

Hardback	228 x155mm	280 pages	90 b/w & colour photographs	6 maps	0 620 22901 2
R140.00	£15.00	US$25.00	C$35.00	A$35.00	NZ$45.00

Aviation

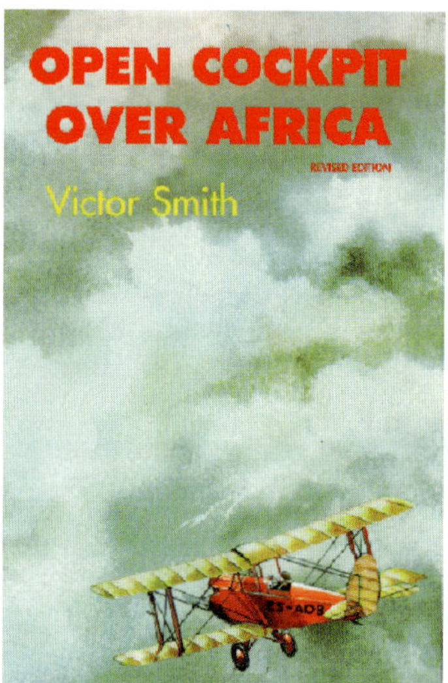

OPEN COCKPIT OVER AFRICA

Victor Smith

The intimate account by one of Africa's pioneering aviators, of what it was like to fly open-cockpit, single-engined aircraft the length and breadth of primitive Africa in the 1930s. A breathtaking and thrilling saga of aerial trail-blazing from London to the Cape and back. It is also of the author's experiences as Beaufighter pilot in the Balkan Air Force during World War II.
– Hammond Innes

Softback	229 x 152mm	196 pages	maps, diagrams 58 b/w illustrations	0 798 50773 X	Faircape Books
R120.00	£15.00	US$25.00	C$35.00	A$35.00	NZ$45.0

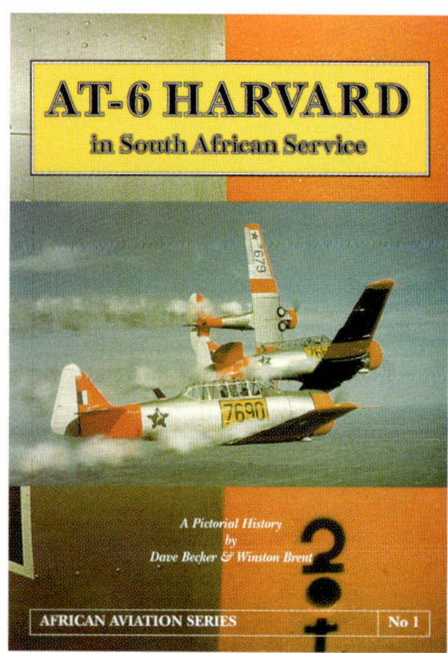

AT-6 HARVARD

– IN SOUTH AFRICAN SERVICE

NEW August 200

Dave Becker and Winston Brent

The Harvard has seen more than 55 years service with the SAAF. This publication is dedicated to the many pilots who owe the success today to having had their initial training on a Harvard. The authors have combined their resources to produce this bo as a tribute.

Softback	285 x 204mm	116 pages	35 colour & 383 b/w photographs	0 958 38802 4	Freeworld Publications
R140.00	£15.00	US$25.00	C$35.00	A$35.00	NZ$45.0

CANBERRA

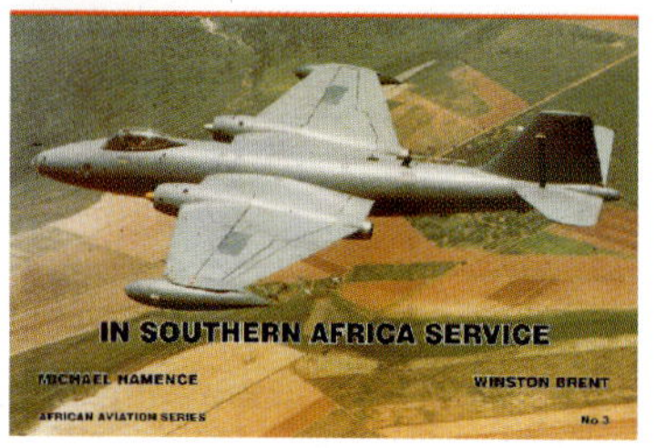

CANBERRA

– IN SOUTHERN AFRICAN SERVICE

Michael Hamence and Winston Brent

The authors have combined their efforts and brought out a tribute to the Canberra in southern Africa service. The Canberra served with distinction in the Rhodesian Air Force and is recorded by Michael Hamence. Winston Brent records its SAAF servi including its operational service over SWA/Namibia and Angola. He lifts the lid on the South African "Nuclear Era" and speculates which aircraft would have carried the "A-bomb". He records the Canberra in an EW role and includes an aerial photograph of the Soviet "spy-ship" *Kapushka.*

Softback	297 x 210mm	96 pages	map, 26 colour & 65 b/w photographs	0 958 38804 0	Freeworld Publications
R140.00	£15.00	US$25.00	C$35.00	A$35.00	NZ$45.0

Aviation

EYE IN THE SKY
– A BRIEF HISTORY OF THE SA POLICE AIR WING

Herman Bosman

A brief history of the SA Police Service Air Wing, recording the use of SAAF aircraft to assist the SAP from the early 1920s to the 1980s when the SAP received their own aircraft and helicopters. He records for the first time the SAP involvement in Rhodesia and SWA/Namibia from 1966.

Softback	297 x 210mm	148 pages	42 colour & 184 b/w photographs	0 958 38805 9	Freeworld Publications
R140.00	£15.00	US$25.00	C$35.00	A$35.00	NZ$45.00

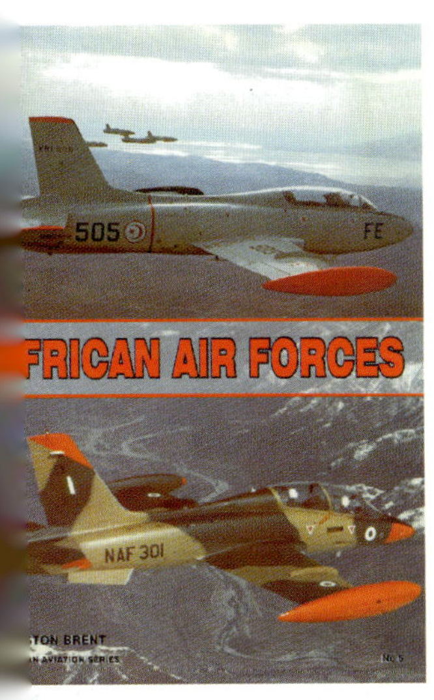

AFRICAN AIR FORCES

Winston Brent

A comprehensive review of the Air Forces of Africa as at 1999, listing all known types of aircraft, including serial numbers, c/ns & fates. Each air force is briefly described. Regarded as the only true reference book on military aircraft in Africa.

Softback	297 x 210mm	218 pages	map, 233 colour & 82 b/w photographs	0 958 38806 7	Freeworld Publications
R265.00	£27.50	US$45.00	C$60.00	A$60.00	NZ$75.00

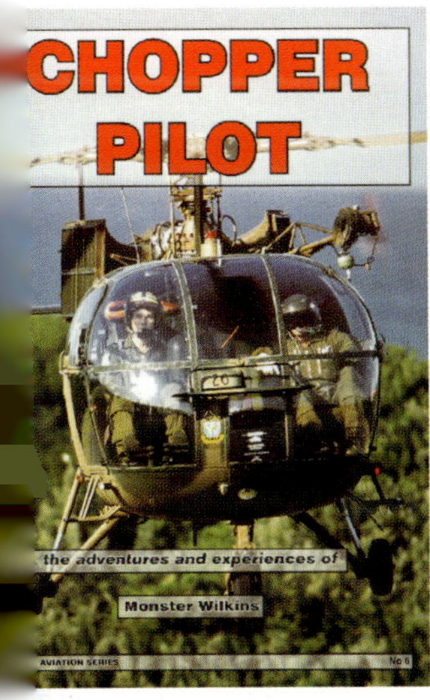

CHOPPER PILOT

Monster Wilkins

The personal experiences and exploits of Monster Wilkins (still serving as a brigadier-general), who is regarded as the SAAF's top helicopter pilot, with over 6,000 hours, of which he has spent in excess of 4,000 hours on his favourite chopper the Alouette III. He details his service in the various operational areas, such as Angola, SWA/Namibia, Rhodesia and Mozambique.

Softback	297 x 210mm	154 pages	39 colour & 192 b/w photographs	0 958 38807 5	Freeworld Publications
R225.00	£27.50	US$45.00	C$60.00	A$60.00	NZ$75.00

Military History & Bush Wars

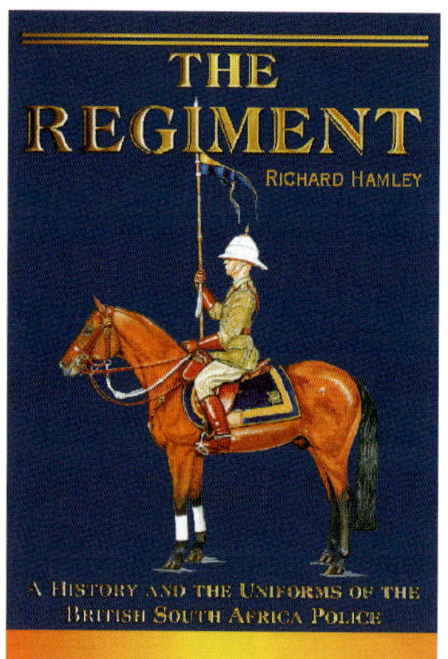

THE REGIMENT

– A History and the Uniforms of the British South Africa Police

Richard Hamley

A stunning coffee-table pictorial production, with the author's own vivid water colour plates included. Traces the developme of this fine colonial military/paramilitary police force in Rhodesia from the 1890s to 1980. Also a Special leather-bound hardback Edition.

Softback	297 x 210mm	approx 160 pages	75 colour plates	2nd Edition	0 620 25394 C
Standard Edition R265.00	£27.50	US$45.00	C$60.00	A$60.00	NZ$75.0
Special Edition R650.00	£65.00	US$100.00	C$160.00	A$160.00	NZ$200.0

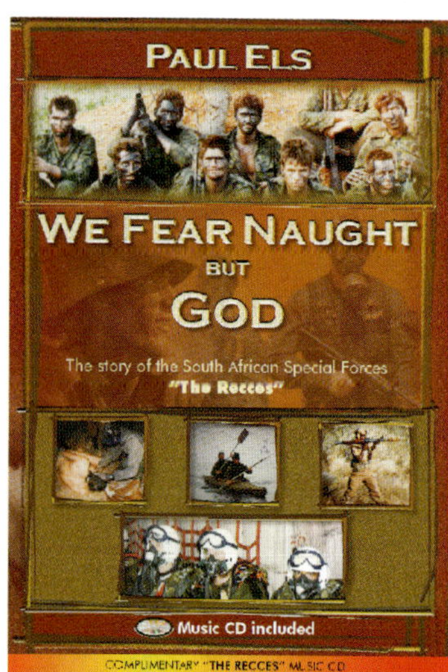

WE FEAR NAUGHT BUT GOD

Paul Els

The story of the South African Special Forces ("The Recces"), from inception in the 1960s to disbandment in 1993. A unique account of one of South Africa's premier units, masters in the art of reconnaissance and clandestine warfare. Pro rata, the highly decorated unit during the wars in Angola and Namibia/SWA.

Includes a free copy of Lourens Fourie's music CD "The Recces"

Softback	222 x 152mm	328 pages	252 b/w photographs	maps	0 620 23891
R140.00	£15.00	US$25.00	C$35.00	A$35.00	NZ$45.0

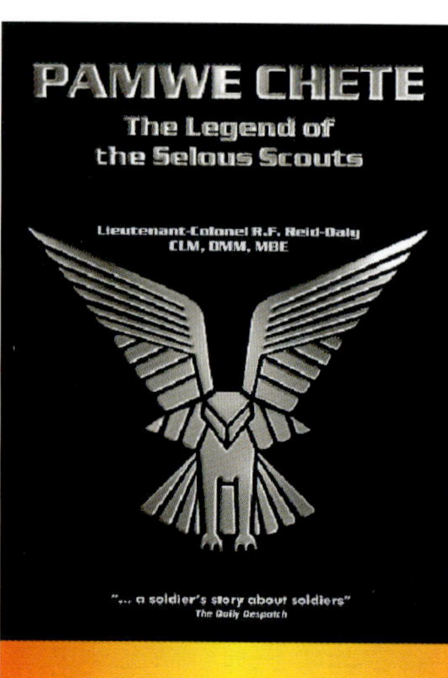

PAMWE CHETE – The Legend of the Selous Scouts

Lieutenant-Colonel Ron Reid-Daly

The revamped, rewritten version of the best-selling *Top Secret War.* With new, previously unpublished material, including the roll of honour and full schedules of citations and wings. New photo sections. The definitive account of this exceptional unit's short but distinguished service in the field of pseudo counter-insurgency operations during the bitter Rhodesian bus war. A classic.

Hardback	228 x 155mm	664 pages	150 b/w illustrations	maps	0 620 2375
R225.00	£27.50	US$45.00	C$60.00	A$60.00	NZ$75.

Military History & Bush Wars

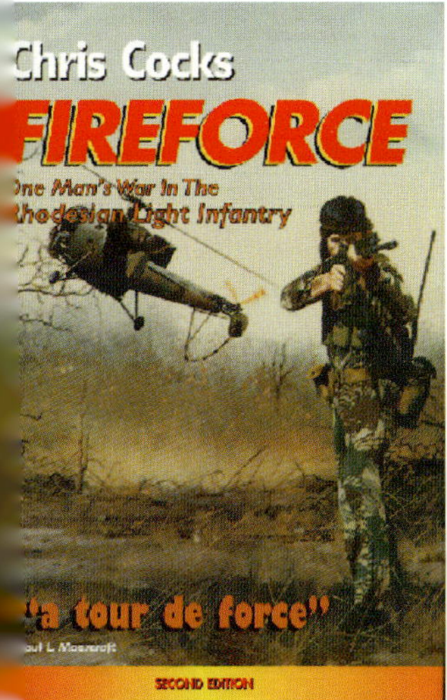

FIREFORCE – One Man's War in the Rhodesian Light Infantry

Chris Cocks

Widely acclaimed as the classic account of counter-insurgency warfare in Africa, as told by the combat soldier "on the ground". The gut-wrenching account of brutal face-to-face combat in the bush, this is not for the squeamish. Has been compared with *Commando* and *Dispatches.* Includes the RLI roll of honour, citations and operational orders, as appendices.

"A tour de force" – Paul Moorcraft

Hardback	228 x 155mm	368 pages	0 620 21573 9	map/sketches 120 b/w & colour photographs	2nd Edition Reprinted 1998, 1999, 2000
R185.00	**£20.00**	**US$35.00**	**C$45.00**	**A$45.00**	**NZ$60.00**

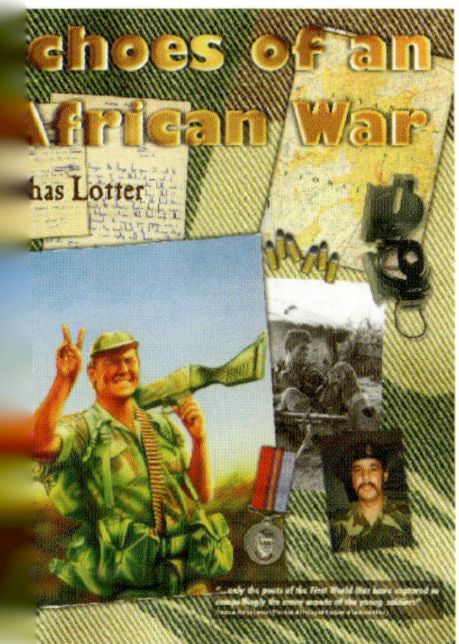

ECHOES OF AN AFRICAN WAR

Chas Lotter

A photographic anthology by Africa's acclaimed soldier-poet. Coffee-table format with alternative pages of haunting poetry, mirrored by some stunning original photography. Also a 150 leather-bound, gilded Limited Edition.

"...only the poets of the First World War have captured so compellingly the many moods of the young soldiers" – Professor Marcia Leveson, President of the English Academy of Southern Africa.

Hardback	330 x 248mm	208 pages	650 colour photographs	0 620 23091 6	
Standard Edition **R295.00**	**£30.00**	**US$50.00**	**C$75.00**	**A$75.00**	**NZ$100.00**
Special Edition **R995.00**	**£100.00**	**US$175.00**	**C$250.00**	**A$250.00**	**NZ$325.00**

ONE COMMANDO – Rhodesia's Last Years, the Guerrilla War

Dick Gledhill

The author's fictionalized account of his service in the elite parachute battalion, One Commando, the Rhodesian Light Infantry, during the height of the guerrilla war. A cracker of a story; action-packed all the way. Well balanced and intriguing.

Softback	178 x 111mm	218 pages	20 b/w photographs	0 646 31036 4	RLI Publishing
R100.00	**£10.00**	**US$17.50**	**C$25.00**	**A$25.00**	**NZ$32.50**

Military History & Bush Wars

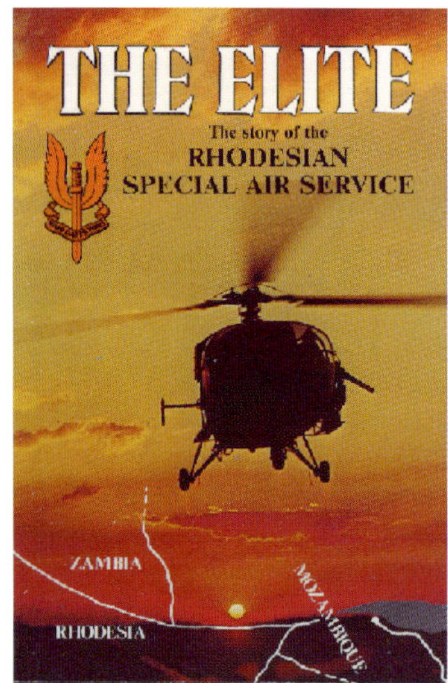

THE ELITE – The Story of the Rhodesian SAS

Barbara Cole

The best-selling account of "C" Squadron, the SAS during the Rhodesian bush war of the 1970s. First published in 1985, thi book is timeless in content and appeal.

"...possibly the most important book about the Rhodesian war from the military side" – Daily Dispatch

Softback	194 x 130mm	461 pages	56 b/w photographs maps	0 620 08517 7	Three Knigh Publishing
R100.00	£10.00	US$17.50	C$25.00	A$25.00	NZ$32.5

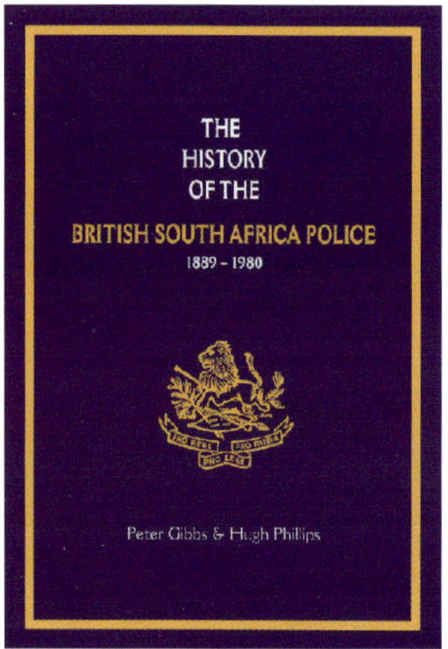

THE HISTORY OF THE BRITISH SOUTH AFRICA POLICE

NEW *November 20*

Peter Gibbs and Hugh Phillips

This definitive volume traces the history of one of the world's finest police forces and how it shaped a nation. The book is contained in two parts: the abridged and updated twin histories by the late Peter Gibbs, from the hardship of settlement i early Rhodesia in 1899 to the outbreak of World War II in 1939, as originally published in his now-scarce early 1970s volu and by Hugh Phillips whose painstaking research covers the equally tumultuous years from 1940 to 1980 when the countr became the fledgling state of Zimbabwe.

Hardback	235 x 155mm	460 pages	72 pages b/w 24 pages colour illustrations	0 646 40119 X	Something of
R285.00	£27.50	US$45.00	C$60.00	A$60.00	NZ$75.